OUT OF CUBA

Memoir of a Journey

REGINA ANAVY

Out of Cuba
Memoir of a Journey

ISBN 978-1-939393-61-6
ISBN 978-1-939393-60-9 (ebook)

Cognitio
Books & Apps

www.cognitiobooks.com

For Ralph, as always

Table of Contents

Ariadne loved Theseus, and she gave him a sword to slay the Minotaur and a thread to unravel, so he could find his way out of the Labyrinth.

Greek myth

Preface

As I stepped off the plane in Havana, I experienced a tinge of anxiety. It had been over thirty years since I had last visited Cuba, and I was no longer the intense political revolutionary I had been in my youth. My first trip was in 1971, when I joined the Venceremos Brigade to cut sugarcane in support of Castro. That adventure had undone me and had left me reeling from disillusionment. I dropped out of radical politics, restructured my life, and integrated shades of gray into my political thinking.

I was now going back to see how the island had changed and what my adult reaction would be. How was I to know that, due to a chance meeting with a stranger, my life was about to be drastically and irrevocably transformed?

What was it about Cuba that drew me in this time? The tropical climate, the music, the sensual ambience? Or was it the Cuban people themselves, full of good humor in the face of adversity, friendly towards Americans, handsome, resourceful? And more than a few of them desperate to get out.

A Cuban friend once told me, "Cuba is like an onion: You think you see the whole reality, but then you start to peel away the layers, one by one, and you discover more realities, until you get down to the core." When I told him I had been to Cuba eight times, he declared, "Then you are almost Cuban!"

But I'm not Cuban, and I doubt that I will ever get down to that core. It's impossible to know everything that is going on in a country where so much is hidden. Even Cubans who have lived on the island all their lives sometimes aren't sure they can decipher the ever-changing reality around them. So how can we non-Cubans ever figure it out? And even if we could figure it out today, tomorrow we would have to start all over again, because things change.

This memoir is my personal journey through the realities I encountered as a tourist, and the realities revealed to me by Cubans who trusted me with information too often kept locked away from foreigners.

I did my best to discover the inner layers of the onion. The process still brings tears to my eyes. As I write this memoir, they are tears of sadness, laughter, and even joy.

Introduction

A Human Memory about a Nation's Trauma

A great kaleidoscope of the most raw, sad, and deplorable Cuban reality: That's what this book is. More than the personal history of the writer, of two Cubans, or some other real people who appear here, it's a hymn to the dreams of a people betrayed by those who seized power. It's a cry of warning to those who today still look at the island with the illusioned glance with which the world contemplated Cuba in the 1970s, wanting to take away something important from what has been fifty-four years of disaster after disaster. It is, simply, a very brief but very human example of those terribly intimate stories that, in exile, are told by almost three million Cubans who have seen themselves forced to flee, as the great Virgilio Piñera would say, from "the cursed circumstance of water on both sides."

Piñera also told Fidel Castro in June 1961, in a meeting where the messianic *Comandante* celebrated with intellectuals in the National Library: "I want to say that I'm very afraid. I don't know why I am but that is all I have to say." And this is the most visible mark of the stories in this book: the fear, as if you live on an island where fear, as well as the waters of the sea, surrounds Cubans everywhere, binding their hands, their dreams, their hopes, their historic defiance. And like Piñera, the majority of those who inhabit the pages of this book feel this fear, which creates an omnipresent, omnipotent danger. A danger that luckily, and perhaps to show us that occasionally happy endings do exist, leaves the protagonists when they are finally far away and safe from the malign source of their fears.

Regina Anavy, like all good journalists, like all good writers, has known how to take the higher road, so her memories of voyage are safe from falling into the usual stereotypes at the hour of writing about the Cuban reality. This absolutely is not a book that analyzes this reality in black and white. It's a book full of nuances, of very objective analyses, of judgments that seek only to establish the limits of possible truths, of anecdotes filled with reflection. And it accomplishes this because each one of the chapters is narrated from a humanistic perspective, where the human beings, their contradictions, problems, fears, vacillations, and doubts constitute the center itself of what is narrated. In the most simple words: This is not a cold analysis of Cuban society and its contradictions, nor is it a personal or family melodrama about a country where every family can tell stories that would make any soap opera pale in comparison. It is, simply, the story of a political illusion (which Regina had, like so many other foreigners who came to Cuba called by the treacherous siren song of a Revolution that pretended to change the world for one that was more humane and just). But it is at the same time a story of the disillusion felt by Cubans and foreigners who struggled, believed, and even died for an ideal that others, clinging to power, betrayed miserably.

This human gaze that Regina throws across particular aspects of the daily, political, and social life of Cubans with whom she had contact on her trips, her persistence in knowing the real Cuban life (which is very different from what is seen from hotels, where most intellectuals, journalists, actors, and artists still stay today, defending the Cuban dictatorship) is what permits her to easily access the door where she finds the truth: the daily suffering, the fears injected by repressive organisms and the iron control of the Communist Party and the State, the dirty channels of snitching as a method of social climbing, the exacerbated satanizing of those who think differently, the loss of dreams and personal ambition, the deceptive propaganda about life in Paradise as the universe falls into the most dehumanized chaos. The dream of knowing that there really is more beyond those waters that crash against the Malecón of Havana or against the beaches and coasts of the entire island; that dream of going anywhere, wherever that may be, but far away, feeling the instability of the unknown but knowing that at least there exists the hope that it could be a better place. Something that certainly reminds us of that maxim that until now never has failed: "The first identifier for measuring a nation's prosperity, the happiness of a people, is the number of persons who want to emigrate somewhere else."

Beyond the clarity of the prose with which Regina Anavy writes these pages, beyond this excellent mural fresco that she offers us about very specific edges of the Cuban story and the Cuban reality, beyond the analysis that she makes, always from the most profound humanism, and beyond the personal history (hers) and the collective history (that of the other protagonists), this book constitutes one of the clearest testimonies of an epoch. It is, without doubt, a book that contributes a vision, a professional and necessary one, about the trauma of a nation: Cuba.

Amir Valle, Berlín, 2013.

Chronology of my Trips to Cuba

- April 1971: Fourth Venceremos Brigade

- October 2003: ElderTreks /Global Exchange People-to-People Reality Tour

- October 2004: Global Exchange Sustainable Communities

- December 2004: Global Exchange Education

- August 2005: Earthwatch American Crocodile Project

- March 2006: Earthwatch American Crocodile Project

- June 2006: Caribbean Medical Transport

- December-January, 2006-2007: Cuban-American Jewish Mission

- October 2008: Bringing Hope Foundation

A Word About my Methods

On every trip to Cuba I kept a detailed daily journal, taking notes during lectures and conversations as they happened, or as soon as I could put pen to paper. I never actually planned to string these journals together into a book, but when I decided to write a compendium of my experiences in Cuba, my notes were invaluable.

When Cubans opened up and shared feelings and thoughts about what they saw going on in their country (and in mine), I transcribed their words verbatim as accurately as I could. I never used a tape recorder or officially interviewed anyone. Understanding that my informants may be reluctant to be identified, and respecting their privacy, I have disguised them by changing their identities, as well as the exact location and timing of our conversations. They know who they are, and they know I am grateful for their honesty and willingness to help me understand their reality.

I

Radical Hubris

In the spring of 1971, the Cuban government asked for volunteers to show support for the Revolution by cutting sugar cane in the Ten Million Ton Harvest. I had earned such impressive radical political credentials by then that I considered my acceptance on the Fourth Venceremos Brigade as a given.

After graduating from the University of California, Berkeley, in 1965, I volunteered to go south with CORE, the Congress of Racial Equality, in the summer, to register African-Americans to vote in St. George, South Carolina. I then joined the domestic Peace Corps, VISTA, to work on a project in Norfolk, Virginia, but this kind of social work was too tame for me. I felt that the way to really effect change was through political action. Moving to Washington, D.C., I became involved in the Free D.C. Movement and worked with SNCC (the Student Nonviolent Coordinating Committee), to press for voting rights for the population of Washington, D.C. After the Black Power movement took over the SNCC office and made it clear they didn't want whites around, I moved on to the Women's Movement, which was just beginning to form. I felt proud to be involved in making American history.

In the spring of 1971, I had a chance to participate in the ultimate Leftist act: going to Cuba, in defiance of U.S. government policy. What hardcore radical could resist? I was annoyed when I found out I had to go through a rigorous application process in order to be accepted. Didn't they know who I was? And who were they to judge me?

A fellow radical grilled me:

"Have you ever done hard physical labor?"

"Yes, I once helped with the haying on a ranch in Montana. I lifted hay bales and tossed them onto a truck."

This sounded impressive, but I neglected to say that I tossed those hay bales for only a short while. It was difficult work, and I was not physically strong. Did I speak Spanish? No. This was an obvious obstacle, but I knew my political credentials were impeccable.

I was ultimately accepted on the Brigade along with six others from the Washington, D.C. area. I did a lot of reading about the Cuban Revolution (the source of the material being the Cuban government itself). Spanish classes were organized, and there were other meetings of the *brigadistas*, but I found it hard to fully commit myself to attending these events, and my lack of interest was noted.

I had a secret motive for wanting to go: Bill, my former boyfriend, now underground with the Weathermen, recently had taken to getting drunk and calling me up at 3:00 a.m. to cast blame.

"If you had married me, I wouldn't be in this situation," he would sob.

I would riposte by saying, "The reason I didn't marry you was I could see where you were headed politically." These conversations went nowhere and usually ended with my hanging up on him, but he continued to call, pleading for some kind of rescue that I couldn't provide.

I wanted to get out of town. I assumed that going away would cement my radical credentials, put me out of reach of Bill, and resolve my inner conflict about continuing in leftist politics. I seriously had my doubts.

Our group of seven included Peter, an attractive man who was a member of the Black Panthers. He and my friend, Judy, had become lovers, so Peter was over at our house a lot. One night he extended an invitation to us: "Would you like to see the 'Voodoo Tapes' that Eldridge made in Algeria?" Peter was referring to Eldridge Cleaver, who had joined the Black Panthers, calling them "voodoo nationalists." They considered themselves Marxists who were part of a revolutionary vanguard. Eldridge was charged with assault and attempted murder after a shoot-out with Oakland police in 1968. He jumped bail and fled to Cuba, along with his wife, Kathleen, but they subsequently became disillusioned with the Cuban revolution, considering it racist, and were now living in Algeria, where he was greeted as a "revolutionary hero" and given a villa in Algiers.

"Sure!" Judy and I said simultaneously. What an opportunity! We felt we must be special: privileged white guests, about to be initiated into a secret world of militant black nationalism that very few got to see.

"You have to be blindfolded," Peter informed us. "We don't want you to know where you are going." So we all piled into a car. Judy and I tied bandanas around our eyes, and we drove around for a while. It seemed like we were going in circles, so we could not pinpoint the location, just like in the movies. Even under torture we would never be able to tell anyone where we had been. Eventually we arrived at a three-story house somewhere in the District. Judy and I were guided up some stairs and were allowed to remove our blindfolds when the front door closed behind us.

Peter ushered us into a room where a group of people, racially mixed and of all ages, were sitting around on the floor. Someone started the video, but to tell you the truth, I don't remember a thing about it, except that Eldridge was talking a lot. The quality of the filming was terrible, and the audio was unintelligible. I didn't recognize any of the people in the room, although I thought I knew everyone in the radical community in Washington. I wanted to converse, but no one would make eye contact with me, or even say hello. There was no joy in the event, and at the same time, it was thrilling to be doing something so illicit.

But I was questioning my involvement with the radical movement. I wasn't sure I really belonged; at the same time I felt guilty about my uncertainty, and I couldn't imagine any other milieu in which I could function. My faith in my own judgment was about to be tested.

II

Counter-Revolutionary

With the warm sunlight of a bright spring day glaring off the silver wings of our charter flight from Mexico City, the Fourth Venceremos Brigade was on its way to Cuba. The Cuban government had invited us and paid for our trip; as far as our own government was concerned, we were breaking the law. The pilot came on the air to announce our arrival in Havana. "Welcome to Cuba, the first free territory in the Americas." Claps and cheers drowned out the sound of our touchdown at the José Martí International Airport. My heart pounded as I watched the cabin door swing open. On the other side of that door lay nine weeks in Communist paradise: seven in the sugarcane fields and two more touring the island.

"*Mis compañeros*," shouted Fernando to the cheering group of visitors. "*¡Bienvenidos!*" He was a Cuban doctor assigned to our group, and his official welcome on behalf of the Cuban government drew return shouts from the crowd of newcomers enthusiastic about being *compañeros*. There were 200 of us North Americans; joining roughly the same number of Cubans and other workers from the Third World. We had come to show solidarity with the Revolution by helping with the sugarcane harvest—the *zafra*.

Piling onto an aged bus, we bounced along the badly paved roads east of the capital, near the town of Aguacate. Our work camp, surrounded by cane fields, consisted of a few thatched-roof, open-air buildings, including a dining hut, an infirmary, a communal bathhouse, and a small refreshment stand where sugarcane was pressed for juice. Canvas tents, scattered haphazardly around the camp, would serve as our new home. Purely functional, each tent was barely big enough for six people. Our beds were nothing but cots arranged in tiers of two, bunk-bed style.

I settled into my tent with five other *compañeras*. Beth, a tall, unsmiling woman in her thirties, was a card-carrying member of the Communist Party from New York City. She carried herself like the genuine article and was appropriately intimidating. She was the only one in our tent who had a watch. The rest of us apparently assumed that time wouldn't matter in revolutionary cane fields. We soon learned that we were on a tight schedule; we especially didn't want to miss meal times.

Amy and Gail were from New York, and both openly lesbian. Amy was short and round; Gail, tall and thin. They made a habit of bad-mouthing other people in the tent late at night, when we were all in our cots and they thought we couldn't hear. Or maybe they wanted us to hear.

My good friend from Washington, D.C., Carole, short, blond, and quiet, was in my tent, along with Nancy, a nurse, who was funny without intending to be.

"I wasn't really sure I should come on this trip," Nancy confided. "I feel guilty about helping with the sugarcane harvest. Sugar is bad for you."

The tent was cramped and uncomfortable. We could barely stand erect, and the air inside was hot and stifling. At night, I had trouble falling asleep. The cots sagged. I was aware of every cough, sniffle, fart, and whisper of gossip. Then someone came up with the bright, space-saving idea of pooling all our clothes, supplies, and toiletries in one suitcase, using it as an open, communal grab bag. We stashed the rest of our luggage under our cots, opened up one large suitcase near the entrance of the tent, and gleefully surrendered our meager possessions—clothing, medications, vitamins, toothbrushes, and toothpaste. Carole and I took this concept to the extreme and decided to share one toothbrush. The group had willingly abolished private ownership, creating our own brand of Revolutionary Communism. In our eyes, individualism and private possession were capitalist conceits and, therefore, unacceptable. From that moment on, we could never find what we wanted when we needed it. And privacy was impossible.

Several *brigadistas* in the camp opted to sleep outside the tents, some even venturing into the fields, laying down sleeping bags on the ground between the rows of cane. They had to contend with the myriad insects, which were everywhere, but they could at least have a semblance of privacy. Couples slept together; more couples formed as the trip wore on.

In front of each tent was a rack of machetes, the tools of our new trade. We each had our own, for which we were responsible. We replaced the machete in the same slot on the rack every day when we returned from the fields. It was important to keep it honed, with a sharp cutting edge. For the seven weeks of our stay in the camp, the machete would be our most valued possession.

The strict schedule provided structure for our days. At sunrise the bright, tropical light filtered into our tent, along with an increase in heat and humidity. We rolled out of our cots and stumbled to the row of sinks outside the bathhouse, where we splashed cold water onto our faces. From there, we headed to the dining hut, lured by the smell of rich, strong coffee. Each of us was handed a shot of espresso in a thimble-sized paper cup, to go with the one cigar we were allowed to take from an open box. Barely awake, we piled into Soviet trucks to be ferried to different spots in the fields. Sometimes the trucks were enclosed; hunched over, we endured the solidarity of this momentary claustrophobia.

For all of us, it was an adventure. We sang inspirational songs about the Revolution, led by our Cuban cohorts. As with the civil rights movement in the U.S. (or maybe any movement), the songs were memorable enough to stay with me across the years. *Adelante, Guerrillero* (Forward, Guerrilla) was one of my favorites; and there was Carlos Puebla's rousing song about Ché Guevara, *Hasta Siempre Comandante* (Farewell, Commander), which we loved. We belted out the refrain by memory:

> *Aquí se queda la clara,*
> *La entrañable transparencia*
> *De tu querida presencia,*
> *Comandante Ché Guevara.*

And of course we sang *Guantanamera*, adapted from *Versos Sencillos*, by José Martí, and popularized by Pete Seeger in the U.S.:

> *Yo soy un hombre sincero*
> *De donde crece la palma,*
> *Y antes de morirme quiero*
> *Echar mis versos del alma.*
> *Guantanamera,*
> *guajira guantanamera,*
> *Guantaname-e-e-e-r-r-r-ra,*
> *guajira guantanamera.*

Arriving in the fields, we were divided into groups for instructions on cane cutting. Sandra, a fierce young Cuban woman, the overseer for my group, shouted out commands. She never once cracked a smile during the lesson. The technique of cutting sugar cane involved holding the cane stalk with one hand and swinging the machete deep at the base of the stalk with the other. As you progressed along the row, you tossed the cut cane into a pile. Another group gathered the cane and stacked it. We alternated between these two tasks. Sandra walked up and down the rows, urging us on in military tones, yelling "¡*Más abajo!*" Cut lower! She had made very clear to us that much of the cane syrup sits low on the stalk, so it was essential that we cut the stalks as low as possible. That meant we had to aim carefully. Occasionally a shinbone would get in the way of the sharp machete blade—this happened even to the Cubans, and having a machete cut became a badge of honor. Tetanus shots were handed out like candy.

The sun was blazing; the work was hot and dirty. Cubans had adopted the Australian method of cutting cane, which meant they burned the fields at night, filling the sky with smoke and flames. The fires against the night sky were a beautiful spectacle, reminding us that the Revolution was going on around the clock and we were doing something important to contribute. The burning accomplished several things. It eliminated the grass and weeds, which made it easier to see the base of the stalk; but more importantly, it burned off the thick leaves lower down on the stalk—the ones with edges as sharp as blades. It also meant that the ground where we toiled was covered with a layer of black, carbonized ash, easily stirred up every time we took a step. The cinders coated our clothing, stuck to our sweaty bodies, and seeped into every exposed pore. I had an especially hard time keeping the particles out of my eyes.

In the morning we had a break, and the kitchen staff brought us a snack of revitalizing yogurt in metal cups. Then it was back to work until lunchtime. We returned to camp in the trucks (same singing routine, with a few shouted slogans thrown in), and headed for the showers, looking like we had survived a brush fire. For those who wanted it, there was always the option of using the laundry service for clean work clothes.

One morning, we found ourselves working in the fields with a contingent from North Vietnam—an unwelcome coincidence to me. I wondered whether the North Vietnamese would show resentment toward us. But they were charming. They explained, "We distinguish between the American people and the American government." As *brigadistas*, we were on their side. So now we found ourselves cutting cane with America's current enemy.

Lunch was always a feast, usually consisting of pork or chicken, black beans and rice, followed by guava paste for dessert—all in plentiful supply. Then it was time to read, talk, or take a siesta, until we went to the fields again in the afternoon. Before each trip, we sat cross-legged on the ground and sharpened our machetes with huge metal files—*limas*. Placing the machete handle under one thigh on the inside, we positioned the blade out and sideways against the other thigh; with both hands, we pushed the *lima* quickly across the cutting edge, in a sweeping motion away from our bodies. This, of course, was just another opportunity for machete wounds—usually to the hand. All these machete injuries meant we were trying really hard ... even if our aim was a bit off.

With all the comings and goings and the general activity in the camp, people often misplaced a shirt or a pair of work pants. This was a source of amazement to one Cuban woman, who commented, "You have so much that you don't care if you lose something. We are always guarding our things."

Following the afternoon work session and another shower, we sat down as a group for dinner. It was pretty much the same as lunch, but with little cakes and other sweets for dessert. Again, the food was plentiful—they wanted to make sure we were well-fueled for the work in the fields. Occasionally, we watched movies at night, in what we called the Palm Theater, where we sat on the ground and leaned against the trunks of felled palm trees. Musicians came into camp to entertain us. Everyone addressed each other as *compañero* or *compañera*—we were really into it.

The Cubans were unlike any group of people I had ever met. They seemed fiercely patriotic and proud of their government, in stark contrast to the current American attitude. I started to feel guilty about this, sensing that the Cubans actually looked down on us for our lack of patriotism. It was clear that they considered us spoiled and self-indulgent. The better they got to know us, the more they were determined to stamp these qualities out of us, through hard work and indoctrination. Only one of the Cuban men had a beard—an anomaly, since only those who actually fought in the Sierra Maestra were supposed to have the right to be *barbudo*; the rest were poseurs. Of course, this latter group included a lot of the North American men.

Social pressure worked subtly in our camp. We were required to show up for work production meetings, where we were lectured on how to increase production. Constructive criticism was encouraged, always done in front of the whole group. On occasion, an important Cuban passed through the camp to give a speech. The arrival was staged. We were expected to drop whatever we were doing, fall out in military fashion, line the path, and clap enthusiastically. I felt like I had joined a cult.

During our siesta one afternoon, I found myself tossing and turning uncomfortably in the sweltering heat of the tent. Unable to sleep, I slipped outside and sat on the ground in front of the machete rack. I planned to file my machete to razor-sharpness, but just then Peter the Panther materialized and sat down directly in front of me. It was the first time we were relatively alone, and I knew he had come with a purpose.

"I've come up with an idea of what we should do when we get back to the U.S.," he whispered conspiratorially. "I want to organize a cadre of black men and white women to work together to build bombs—to engage in strikes against the government."

My jaw dropped. I really didn't know what to say. *Great idea, sign me up? Are you insane? Come on, Peter, tell me the truth: You're really an FBI agent, aren't you?* As it was, I said nothing; maybe I was too shocked. Peter apparently didn't really expect a response. He just smiled, stood up, and went off to recruit other unsuspecting white women. I heard later that he ran his idea past the Cubans. Peter must have thought they would be impressed with his revolutionary zeal. Apparently, they considered him crazy and ignored him; he became a pariah for the last weeks we were there.

Ironically, years later, I would learn that the Venceremos Brigade was considered an ideal recruiting ground for Cuban intelligence to place agents in the U.S. At the time, I was convinced that the Cuban government's motivation for having us there was its mistaken impression that we, on the Left, had more political power than we actually did. I assumed the Cubans paid for our trip because they imagined we would go home and educate people about the "true" nature of the Revolution. Of course, this meant they were sure we'd all return lauding the Revolution, or that they would persuade us to come over to their side.

Judy, meanwhile, had broken up with Peter. I wasn't surprised: I had often heard them yelling at each other at night out in the fields. Why had she hooked up with him in the first place? "As protection," she told me. "I was scared of going on this trip." Now that she was free of him, she blossomed. She bragged openly about how the Cuban men were attracted to her, and she took pains to look well-groomed every day, unlike most of us. Judy had brown hair, blue eyes, a winning smile, and a full, curvy body—the kind that Cuban men found sexy. She always made sure she got clean work clothes from the laundry during our midday break, and she was expert at flirting. In short, she had the good sense to take care of herself. This struck me as rather individualistic of her. She and I had been close friends before the trip; now I felt abandoned. Judy's best friend and sidekick was now Ellen, a beautiful young woman with long, dark hair. Their whispered confidences made me feel left out.

After Judy broke up with Peter, she chose Wilfredo. He was Afro-Cuban, an agricultural student whom we all liked. Wilfredo was calm and sweet; he seemed sincerely concerned about other people—the very embodiment of our ideal of what a true revolutionary should be.

The more I worked in the fields, the taller and more overwhelming the sugarcane seemed. I felt dwarfed in comparison—a surrealistic feeling that I attributed to the heat, lack of sleep, and my inner turmoil, caused by my increasing doubt about the Revolution and the guilt this doubt engendered in me.

About four weeks into the trip, Carole decided she had had enough. "Let's see if we can leave early," she suggested. We went immediately to find Sandra. We were utterly unaware of the complicated logistics that were involved with such a request.

Sandra let us have it: "I thought the two of you were revolutionaries," she hissed, putting an end to the discussion. This was not summer camp, where your parents could come pick you up. What were we thinking?

By now, the initial courting period of good behavior and enthusiasm had worn off. We cane-cutters were hot and exhausted, and a less cooperative side of our nature was emerging. Gone were the idealists who loved humanity in the abstract; we were now malcontents, increasingly intolerant of individuals.

It began with arguments among the different political factions in the camp. We were all there: the Women's Liberation Movement, the Puerto Rican Independence Movement, Black Panthers, the Gay Liberation Movement, and any other movement you could think of—a full spectrum of the American left in microcosm. Everyone seemed to be competing with each other to be the most revolutionary in an effort to win approval from the Cubans. In the U.S., these groups were separated by self-interest, ethnicity, gender, and geography; here, we were all thrown together—side by side under arduous physical circumstances, without the creature comforts we were used to at home.

Early on, the Cubans made it very clear they did not approve of the gay *brigadistas*, whom they considered counter-revolutionary.

This was their catchword; to be branded counter-revolutionary was the biggest insult imaginable. For non-Cubans, it meant being ostracized; for Cubans, it meant jail. At first, I was naïve and surprised at the Cuban attitude toward Gay Liberation. Then I became appalled that so many *brigadistas* were parroting this attitude, adhering strictly to the party line. And for what? Simply to impress their hosts? The gay *brigadistas* were soon shunned by Cubans and North Americans alike. To me, the gay *brigadistas* were the underdogs—downtrodden like those with whom we supposedly pledged solidarity. And as I continued to hang out with my gay friends, I found myself becoming an outcast. People were now openly depressed. The photos I took of my gay friends showed scowling, tense faces.

Rumors of counter-revolutionary behavior crackled in the air and spread through the camp. "Why are you taking so many photos?" someone challenged me. I had acquired a second-hand Leica before the trip. It never occurred to me that I, with my radical credentials, would become suspect. Now I was being looked at and avoided like I was an agent for the C.I.A.

I had been hanging out—platonically—with one particular Cuban man. Alberto was slim and pale, with curly red hair, hazel eyes, and freckles—rather cute, but not really my type. He originally sought me out, and we began eating meals together and talking. But when I tried to hug him, he rejected me with this explanation: "They warned us before you came that you would attempt to poison our minds against the Revolution. They told us you would try to seduce us." So much for all the solidarity. This was just one more concept that was turning out to be a sham. Considering that many of the Cuban men had seduced the North American *brigadistas*, I found his comment hypocritical. Still, I felt hurt that Alberto would no longer sit with me or talk to me. My sense of isolation increased; I had been "marginalized."

Nonetheless, I managed to get up every morning, go to the fields, and cut cane, though my heart and mind were no longer in it. I was merely marking time, and I was having an existential crisis. I couldn't shut off the reality of Cuba, which was turning out to be very different from my romantic fantasy. I tried to deny my perceptions; they made me feel guilty. *There must be something wrong with me for not being able to go along with the program.* I blamed myself, and the effect was jarring to my soul. *Am I doomed to rebel against any kind of authority? Don't I have any core beliefs?*

It was clear to me, for example, that individual rights were not recognized in Cuba. Everything was geared toward the collective in a kind of numbing, group-think ideology. Nor was there anything subtle about the disdain for the U.S. One Cuban newspaper, *Granma*, spelled "America" with a "k." If nothing else, this offended my literary sensibilities. If the Revolution couldn't even spell correctly, how could it be taken seriously?

The realization that my thinking about Cuba was a total self-delusion began to creep in, even as I tried to deny it. My identity was at stake; it felt shattered, and I didn't know how to put it back together. There were, indeed, certain values that I held in common with the Revolution—the empowerment of women, the demand for a literate society, health care, and education. But now I had my doubts about the sincerity of the Cuban rhetoric. There was a self-righteous, puritanical, and downright intolerant atmosphere in the camp that I found disheartening, if not frightening. Too many of us Americans seemed to be denying our own identities, wanting to adapt to the Cuban idea of who we should be. We arrived as a bunch of pot-smoking lefties who welcomed gay people into our struggle back home. Now we were supposed to be taking lessons from the Cubans on how to be homophobic, undemocratic, and militaristic. There was something seriously wrong here, and I was not the only one who felt this way.

Nancy the nurse confided that she also felt dismayed by what she saw going on in camp. "I've had it with the Movement. When I go back home, I'm just going to concentrate on my job and forget about politics." Such a whispered conversation, such thoughts on our part, made us what we had never thought we would be: counter-revolutionary.

Finally, our stint in the cane fields was over. We began the second phase of our Cuban adventure: a two-week tour of the island. We constituted a cumbersome mob traveling around by bus, 200 *brigadistas* plus our Cuban handlers. We spent the first few days going to dairy farms to learn about the insemination of cows—and I don't mean artificially. The Cubans were very proud of their cattle-breeding program, centered on Holstein bulls imported from Canada.

It soon became a running joke: "What are we doing today?"

"Going to watch the cows fuck!"

Ellen had her own little adventure. Having gotten pregnant by a Cuban, she was whisked off to a clinic for a quickie abortion. When she returned, she was visibly upset.

Getting off the bus in a village one night, we found ourselves immediately surrounded by a crowd of young men. They were yelling for attention, trying to talk to us; it felt like an assault. Our handlers ordered us to get back on the buses, quickly. We complied—with a mob chasing after us! I wasn't sure what was going on; these Cubans seemed to be asking for our addresses in the U.S. "Ah," I thought. "Pen pals." I scribbled my address hastily on a scrap of paper and tossed it out the bus window to a rabble of raised hands.

Were we being protected from them or vice versa? Our aged bus peeled out of the village, speeding away from the danger. From that point onward, we were forbidden from speaking to the locals unless it was arranged in advance. Our tour guides apologized: These rural Cubans had not been schooled in how to deal with foreigners. Probably the young men asking for our addresses were hoping we would help them find a way off the island.

Privacy was something I didn't realize I missed until the day I suddenly reclaimed it. Cutting out early from a lecture at our hotel, I headed for the shower—hot water was available for the first time. Luxuriating in the feeling, my reverie was soon interrupted by another woman yelling at me to get out of the shower so she could have some hot water, too. We had become competitive and nasty with each other over scarce resources.

The culmination of the tour was a forced march in the Sierra Maestra, where we were supposed to be reliving the guerilla experience. Up and down the hills we hiked with our Cuban escorts urging us on. One day, instead of walking, we were told to run. Even Judy had had enough by this point. She pointed to a plant growing alongside the path: "Look! It's marijuana!" I could tell she was tempted to pluck it from the ground and smoke it. But here came Sandra again, shouting sadistically at us to run faster. Who were we soft North Americans kidding? We were not guerilla material.

One day we stopped at the shack of a rural *guajiro*, and the conversation went something like this:

"Hi, we are members of the Venceremos Brigade."

"Please come in and have some coffee."

The man ordered his wife to make us *cafecitos*. She scowled as she filled the small espresso pot and put it on the gas. She wouldn't look at us. Conversation was sparse. It didn't occur to us that we were probably using up their whole week's ration of coffee. We considered it an honor for them to have such distinguished guests. They had no choice but to serve us—no matter how they felt.

At the end of the trip we were shipped back to Canada in the hold of a freighter. A couple of women in our group had fallen in love with Cuban men and stayed behind—something I couldn't imagine doing. My core identity, my belief in radical politics, to which I had dedicated my life for years, had been shattered. I was distraught and deeply concerned that if my core had been that fragile, made of glass rather than of steel, what did that say about my commitment? I had essentially lost my religion—the Movement—and I felt it happened not by choice but rather by the undeniable evidence of its betrayal in a land that many of us once considered holy.

The problem was that I couldn't yet conceive of what would replace it. Being a radical had defined me intellectually, emotionally, and socially for a long time. I felt lost, paralyzed, terrified of the future. I no longer had the energy even to pretend to participate in the merriment shared by the rest of the group on the journey home. While they played card games, chatted, and laughed up on deck, I curled up in my bunk in the ship's hold, too exhausted to stay awake, too disturbed to sleep. Occasionally, when I felt better, I stood up on deck, looking out over the rail at the water, resisting the impulse to jump overboard. I was experiencing a severe depression.

The boat trip took four or five days; I don't really remember, as time no longer held any meaning for me. Finally, we came across the Canadian border at St. Johns, New Brunswick.

"Quick," someone warned. "The customs officials are taking away our T-shirts." We ducked into the bathrooms to pile on another layer of clothing over our orange Venceremos Brigade T-shirts. One *brigadista* had stolen his machete and was trying to get it through Customs. We also had a lot of those little Soviet pins with portraits of Stalin and Lenin.

I honestly didn't need a souvenir of the trip. I had made the decision that it was time for me to drop out of radical politics. I didn't realize it at the time, but I had experienced the same disillusionment felt by many Cubans who initially supported Castro and then realized that revolutionary propaganda can be wrapped in a multitude of evils.

I went back to living in Washington, D.C., and one day there was a knock at the door. Two men, dressed in suits and ties, presented their credentials.

"We're from the F.B.I. We'd like to talk to you about your trip to Cuba."

"I know my rights, and I prefer not to talk to you."

Years later, when I requested my F.B.I. file under the Freedom of Information Act, it was noted that my behavior on that day was "polite." The agents never again returned to question me. Clearly, I had been put on a list in my own country, but there were no real consequences. I didn't lose my passport or my right to vote. I wasn't fined. I didn't go to jail. It occurred to me that if this were Cuba, things would have been a lot different.

Ironically, this Solidarity-with-the-Revolution trip had the opposite effect of what was probably its intention. It made me really patriotic, more appreciative of the freedoms we take for granted in America. Clearly, I was not a good candidate for brainwashing. From a revolutionary standpoint, I was a failure.

III

Decision Time

Years went by. I left Washington, D. C. in 1972 and moved back to California. My involvement with the Radical Left became a distant memory. My political commitments were now boringly mainstream and conventional, within the system. I had matured enough to perceive reality in shades of gray, rather than as all black or all white. I married Ralph in 1986, and we ran a business out of our home in San Francisco. We traveled frequently. Life was good.

In the summer of 2003, I received a brochure from a Canadian tour company named ElderTreks that was organizing a tour to Cuba under Global Exchange's "people-to-people" license. Global Exchange runs a lot of tours to offbeat destinations, calling them "reality tours." How I got on the mailing list for this trip I don't know. I had never heard of ElderTreks, but their catalogue was intriguing. Also, one of my best friends had gone to Cuba recently and raved about her trip.

Many people don't know that Americans can travel to Cuba legally, if they have a license from the Office of Foreign Assets Control (OFAC), an agency of the U.S. Department of the Treasury. The license is really just a piece of paper with a number, which you present to the Customs and Immigration officials when you return to the U.S., proving that you have had official government permission to travel to Cuba for a specified period of time. Essentially, having this piece of paper means that you don't have to lie on the form you fill out when you return to the U.S., the one that asks you what countries you've visited since leaving. Having that OFAC license number means you can truthfully write down *Cuba*; this detail is important because it's a serious offense to lie to an Immigration official.

In 2003, the licensing rules for travel to Cuba were still pretty liberal; travelers could even bring back anything considered *educational* from Cuba, such as CDs, artwork, and books. But many of the licenses were expiring at the end of the year, and it was rumored that not many would be renewed; touring Cuba would soon become illegal. So, thirty-two years after my first, ill-fated trip, I thought about going back, legally this time, to see what had become of the island, and what had become of my perceptions about the island. I was apprehensive, for I was no longer in the mood to be harangued about the wonders of the Revolution. Traveling with a small group on a legal tour sounded appealing, as did staying in comfortable hotels rather than a work camp, but I wanted to make sure it was the right decision.

The Commonwealth Club in San Francisco was sponsoring a symposium on Cuba, and I looked forward to hearing various points of view concerning the issue of travel to the island. The panel of speakers included only one person who opposed travel to Cuba, and I especially wanted to hear his side of the story before making up my mind. I already knew the arguments in favor of traveling to the island: Americans should have the right to travel freely anywhere in the world; we would be sharing our ideals of freedom and democracy by going there; we would be helping the Cuban people, not the Castro government.

I arrived at the symposium early and was lucky to find a seat in the packed auditorium. Across the aisle from me were Medea Benjamin, the founder of Global Exchange, and people from the Left. There were also Cuban-Americans in the crowd. The panel consisted of Wayne Smith, the former U.S. Mission Chief in Havana and head of the Center for International Policy; Delvis Fernández-Levy, the President of the Cuba American Alliance Education Fund; Kirby Jones, the President of the U.S.-Cuba Trade Association; and Frank Calzón, the Executive Director of the Center for a Free Cuba. Lewis Dolinsky, a former foreign affairs columnist for the *San Francisco Chronicle*, was the moderator.

Wayne Smith, who also ran a travel agency that sent people to Cuba, took the position that the U.S. embargo did no good, and the U.S. would effect more change by allowing Americans to travel freely to Cuba. Delvis Fernández-Levy put forth the idea that the embargo had a debilitating effect on Cuban citizens and was unethical. Kirby Jones made a surprise announcement.

"Guess what? There IS no embargo: Cuba now engages in trade with the U.S. for agricultural products, which are exempt from the embargo, as are medical supplies, and humanitarian aid." Basically, what all these speakers were saying was that it was time for the U.S. to engage with Cuba, and traveling there should be allowed. There was no mention of any responsibility on the part of the Cuban government to do anything different to encourage us to connect. The burden was ours alone, as if every failure of the Cuban government could be traced back to U.S. policy.

Then Frank Calzón spoke. "I'm greatly outnumbered, because I'm the only one on this panel who is opposed to Americans traveling to Cuba." He went on to explain that Cuba engaged in "tourist apartheid." Cubans weren't allowed in the tourist hotels, and they didn't receive the same food or medical treatment that tourists received. Under the dual currency system, tourists had to change their money into "convertible" pesos, which they could use in special "dollar" stores where Cubans couldn't afford to shop, since they got paid in a different currency that was worth much less. The average Cuban salary was twelve U.S. dollars/month. "If you were opposed to traveling to South Africa because of the racial apartheid," Calzón concluded, "you should think twice about going to Cuba."

I listened attentively, but it soon became impossible to hear, because, as if on cue, Medea Benjamin and her entourage leapt out of their seats and began screaming at Frank Calzón: "You're not telling the truth! You don't know what you're talking about!" Those of us who wanted to hear Calzón's viewpoint didn't have a chance. The same thing happened when it came time for questions from the audience. I had a very simple question: *Who is in line to take over after Fidel?* But I didn't get a chance to ask it because too many people jumped in line ahead of me in order to continue berating Calzón.

Obviously, these demonstrations had been orchestrated in advance. Just as I finally reached the microphone, the moderator pulled the plug. The event was officially over. I felt frustrated, and I decided to hang around to see if I could get close to the podium in the hopes of having a rational conversation with one of the panelists.

A crowd gathered around Calzón, and I heard a woman thank him for coming to speak. A man who was planning to travel to Cuba asked what he should bring. "Soap," Calzón answered. "Bring small bars of soap."

IV

Surreality Tour

Our group of sixteen flew into Havana from Cancún, arriving at José Martí International Airport just before midnight. Collecting our baggage, we piled onto a bus for the trip into Old Havana. There was activity in the street, even at this late hour. As soon as we deplaned, Cubans approached us and asked, in English, "Where are you from? Do you love Cuba?" Our hotel, the Hotel Florida, was an elegant colonial mansion across from a park. Marlene, my assigned roommate, was amazed.

"I really didn't expect to see people walking around freely on the street like this."

"Why not?" I asked, thinking, *people stay up late in tropical countries.*

"Because it's a Communist country," she replied. "I went to the Soviet Union once, and it was nothing like this. People were afraid to talk to us, and no one was out on the street."

Our room in the hotel was embarrassingly luxurious, quite a contrast to sleeping in a stuffy tent in the middle of a cane field with five other people. We had two huge beds, cable television, and a beautiful armoire. The bathroom was colossal, with a marble tub and sink. We had an ample supply of shampoo and soap, emery boards, shower caps, and sewing kits—a real haul. The air conditioning kept us cool; the hot water was plentiful. Were we really in a Third World country?

We went down to the hotel dining room for an ample breakfast with plentiful *café con leche*. Everyone in the hotel was helpful, except for the clerk at the front desk. When I asked him for my own room key, he ignored me, but later in the day I got one from a female desk clerk. Steve, our Canadian leader, told me it could be because of the *macho* Cuban culture: They don't take females seriously. But I think it actually had more to do with my not offering him a tip.

On the first day of the tour, we met our local guide, Teseo, a tall, lanky man around forty years old. He had short, jet-black hair, a thin face, and beautiful green eyes that twinkled with humor and intelligence. Teseo spoke English very well, with a charming Cuban accent, in a deep voice. He chain-smoked and was constantly in motion, talking on his cell-phone or arranging things for our group.

Our bus driver, Juan Carlos, a very large man, also in his forties, was handsome and flirtatious. He took my hand to help me on and off the bus and looked deeply into my eyes with his light blue ones, smiling suggestively. I always smiled back at him, enjoying the attention. Later we discovered that he had a girlfriend almost everywhere along the tourist route, and we noticed empty beer cans littering the bus in the morning. Someone began calling him "Don Juan Carlos" and the name stuck. "Race-Car Carlos" would have been more like it, as he drove alarmingly fast and passed every other vehicle on the road.

"Don't worry," Teseo reassured us. "We don't have insurance companies here, so every one drives carefully. He isn't going to commit suicide." Still, there were some close calls, by our standards. It was all part of the living-dangerously fun of being in Cuba.

After breakfast on Day One, we had an obligatory orientation from a Global Exchange representative. Our guides groused about this; I was not sure why. The Global Exchange rep, Leslie, turned out to be an American woman, an attorney for Global Exchange, who had been living in Cuba for seventeen years, working for Radio Havana. She was very pretty, showing off her legs and other attractions in tight shorts and a T-shirt. She asked each of us to talk about why we came on the trip, so I mentioned that I had been on the Fourth Venceremos Brigade. She perked up. "I was on the Brigade also, in 1979." I wanted to talk to her further, but there was no time for an in-depth conversation.

Then came the official briefing from Carlos, a teacher at the Institute of International Studies. Teseo introduced him, dismissively: "This guy was my boss at the Foreign Ministry. He will give you the official line, and then I will tell you what's really going on." His bravery surprised me. Carlos began his spiel, which was entirely predictable, a run-down of how terrible American Imperialism was and how free the Cubans are after Fidel Castro began running things in 1959. After he and Leslie left, I overheard Teseo and Steve doing a post-mortem on the official opening of our tour, laughing about the Global Exchange rep.

"Leslie doesn't have a clue about what's really happening in Cuba."

"Well, how could she? She lives in Miramar." Miramar, an upper-class neighborhood, was where the elite lived. Most of the foreign embassies in Havana were in this area.

"She must be sleeping with someone high-up," Steve concluded.

Old Havana was a marvelous pastiche of colonial architecture, declared a World Heritage site by UNESCO. The buildings that couldn't be saved were torn down and parks built in their place to provide more greenery. Amongst the restored buildings we saw shabby apartments with clothes hanging on lines outside the windows.

"Havana has a lot of housing problems," Teseo told us. Many families crowd into one small apartment. And look at this." He pointed out a tangle of electrical wires. "Cubans tap into the grid illegally. There are an estimated 200,000 illegal immigrants in Havana, Cubans who don't have official permission to leave their place of residence."

As we strolled down the streets, beggars followed us, calling softly, *jabón, jabón*. It was the first time in all my travels I had heard people begging for soap. Why? I asked Teseo.

"Cubans get one bar of laundry soap every two months. Even a tiny hotel soap is a prize."

I was forming my own impressions after a couple of days, comparing them to what I had experienced in 1971. Cubans now seemed freer on certain levels. Men could have long hair or be openly gay. People no longer seem concerned with catchwords like *revolutionary* and *counter-revolutionary*; they were just trying to survive.

In 1971 if you asked them, "How goes *la lucha?*" you were asking about the struggle against U.S. imperialism. Now the word *lucha* meant the daily struggle to find food.

Cubans no longer admitted that the government economic and political system was communism. They called it socialism and complained that the government didn't really provide a social safety net. Instead of *socialismo* they talked about *sociolismo*, meaning that the system worked only insofar as *socios*, buddies, helped each other out. Cubans did still talk about *el bloqueo*, a misnomer for the embargo, but they blamed it only partially for their plight. In whispered conversations they told me they no longer respected Fidel. It wasn't that they disagreed with the original aims of the Revolution. It was more a case of *Why didn't the Revolution become what they told us it would be? Why didn't it give us the life we were promised?*

The Cubans were friendly, and wanting to talk, they often approached us. They seemed starved for information about the outside world. Everyone wanted to know where I had traveled and how I found other countries compared to Cuba.

Back on the bus, Teseo talked about the media in Cuba. "There are three government-controlled television stations and three government-controlled newspapers. But if you really want to know what's going on, you can go to a bar where tourists go and watch CNN. So when there's something important happening, like the Marines getting ready to invade, you will know about it." Teseo smiled and paused for effect. "This is one of the many contradictions of Cuban society."

He pointed out that there were no commercials on television or radio, but in fact there were, not for consumer products, but for the Revolution itself. Billboards were everywhere proclaiming *We shall win, Socialism or death*, and other slogans that added to the sensation of being back in the Fifties with the Cold War still raging. This and all the 1950s automobiles in the street created the general feeling of being in a time warp. It was bizarre and amusing at the same time. Amusing because we knew we could leave. The Cubans couldn't.

Day Two, and we were on our way to Viñales, west of Havana. As we drove, Teseo continued to provide us with information on Cuban history and customs.

"Okay, medical care is supposedly free, but in reality, you have to pay a bribe to a doctor, in the form of goods or dollars. For example, we might go to a doctor and say, 'Look, I have this great pair of shoes, but they are too tight for me. Perhaps you can use them.' And the doctor will say, 'Thank you. Now what can I do for you?' Or an X-ray technician might tell you the machine is broken, until you come up with a few dollars. This is the way it works here, and it's humiliating to everyone."

Teseo was challenging us to look beneath the surface of things. He seemed to be constantly trying to tell us something, if only we would really pay attention.

There were two levels of speech going on: the canned, tour-guide rhetoric and the hint at his real feelings, often told in the form of a joke. As we passed the plaza in front of the U.S. Special Interests Section, for example, Teseo pointed out the statue of José Martí, the Cuban hero, holding Elián González, the child whose name was in the news for months after he was the only survivor of an ill-fated raft trip by Cubans trying to escape to Florida. Elián was ultimately returned to his father in Cuba by order of the U.S. government, a victory for Cuba. The statute showed Martí pointing accusingly at the U.S. Special Interests Section. "Martí is supposed to be showing attitude," explained Teseo, "but we Cubans say he's actually telling Elián, 'This way to a visa!'"

I listened closely, taking copious notes on everything Teseo said, and I laughed at all his jokes. His humor reminded me of Jewish humor: dark, and founded on pain. Someone once told me that Cubans are considered the "Jews of the Caribbean," and now I was beginning to understand why.

I also felt that Teseo and I "got" each other, and I appreciated the fact that he was not afraid to challenge me: "This one thinks she can speak Spanish," he joked, after one of my pathetic attempts to say something. He teased me like the brother I had always wanted. By the end of the trip, I was putting my arm around him, calling him my *hermano*, and telling him I wanted to adopt him.

Later, after we really become friends, I asked him why he dared to be so outspoken about what was really going on in Cuba. "Because I knew you were all sophisticated and well-traveled, and I wanted you to respect me," was his answer. At the time, some of us expressed concern that he would get into trouble. "It's true that there are microphones everywhere," he replied, "but I don't worry about it because the batteries are probably dead."

I drove Teseo nuts asking a lot of questions, which he patiently answered. Naturally I was interested in my old "job" in Cuba. I knew that the vaunted Harvest of Ten Million Tons had been a failure. Teseo told me that sugar production was down by fifty percent, and the sugar mills (never modernized even though the Soviets subsidized production for years) were being shut down. Cuba was now importing sugar, and tourism had become the main industry.

The only way we could spend money in Cuba was to exchange our American dollars for Cuban convertible pesos, known as CUCs (rhymes with "nukes"). One CUC was worth about eighty American cents, and the "regular" money, the Cuban peso, *la moneda nacional*, with which Cuban workers were paid, was worth a lot less. It took twenty-six Cuban pesos to make up one CUC. And no one wanted tips in Cuban pesos. One of the perks for Cubans working in the tourist industry was the opportunity to get their hands on CUCS, which they could then spend in the dollar stores, where most of the things worth buying were found.

"This creates a trickle-up economy," explained Teseo, "with hotel workers earning more money than professionals. Bribery has become a way of life. Doctors sometimes moonlight as cab drivers, paying someone for a taxi license. And it works this way: Let's say a Spanish company wants to build a hotel. The Cuban government keeps fifty-one percent ownership but does not spend any of its own money to build the hotel. The Spanish company agrees to hire Cuban workers and pays them in dollars, but the payment has to go through the Cuban government, which pays the workers 260 Cuban pesos a month and keeps the rest. This is a win-win situation all the way around, a splendid deal for the hotel owners.

"There are no independent labor unions or collective bargaining here, and no taxes. However, given the lack of motivation among the Cuban workers, who are being paid peanuts, the Spanish have to come in every so often and bribe their employees by paying them under the table. This is the only way the hotels could have a semblance of functioning. We have a joke in Cuba: The government pretends to pay us, and we pretend to work."

On our second day in Pinar del Rio, we engaged in a "covert" operation engineered by Steve. We pretended to be looking at a view from the top of a hill, then quickly ran down a path through the forest to sneak onto a tobacco farm. Enrique, the tobacco farmer, was required to produce a quota of tobacco for the government and had to accept the government price. If he exceeded his quota, he was allowed to keep the rest. "I actually mix up the different layers of the leaves before taking them to the government market," he admitted. "That way I can keep the higher-quality leaves myself."

He showed us his tobacco plants and described how they are grown and dried in a shed. On the back porch of his house, he demonstrated the technique of cigar rolling and gave each of us one cigar. Whoever wanted another one could pay him a dollar. This was less than we would pay in a government store and more than he could earn legally. When I referred to ourselves as *"norteamericanos"* he corrected me: *"Somos todos AMERICANOS."* He gave me a big hug.

The fact that we donated over-the-counter medications, toys, and other goods, leaving them tactfully on a bed in one of the rooms, helped to cement the warmth. In turn, the family served us some snacks. I asked Teseo if it would be rude to refuse something to eat. "Just be yourself," he counseled, which sounded like good, brotherly advice.

We spent the whole afternoon hanging out with Enrique and his family, drinking sugar-cane juice and coffee, without any pressure to do anything else. Some people went horseback riding. I played with the cat and the children. The men sat on the porch and smoked their *tabacos.*

Marlene approached me. "Do you realize that Teseo has been talking to some people about getting out of Cuba"? In the middle of nowhere, away from the eyes and ears of Havana, he apparently felt even freer to speak his mind. I was not surprised, but I felt hurt that he had not talked to me. Were we not friends? Or was it a matter of *macho* Cuban pride? I was just a woman; what could I do? I think Marlene knew by telling me this that I would take the plunge and approach Teseo myself. She was right.

"Teseo, can we talk privately?"

Sitting apart from the others, speaking softly, Teseo expressed his long-held desire to leave the island. "As soon as I was a teenager and figured out what was going on here, I knew I had to get out. I kept asking my parents questions about why things were the way they were in Cuba. When I asked them why Ché Guevara went to Bolivia, they told me that Fidel sent Ché there to get rid of him. Ché was too popular, and he wanted to create a different model for socialism, something that was more Chinese than Russian. At that point I began to have doubts about what I was being taught in school.

"The rumor now is that Castro's health is failing and he has become isolated and too dependent on his handlers, who tell him what he wants to hear rather than the truth. One joke goes like this: Fidel's people tell him a certain pig farmer has increased his piglet production to twenty-four pigs, when in fact it's only twelve. 'Oh,' says, Fidel. 'That's wonderful, let's take half and let him keep half.' So the farmer gets nothing.

"Here's another one: There's a man who can talk to God by telephone. His friends want him to ask God how long Fidel will live. What with cholesterol drugs and cloning, they fear that Fidel might live forever. The man phones God, asks the question, then puts back the receiver. 'What happened?' his friends ask. 'God hung up.' In other words, not even God knew how long Fidel would live.

"Have you heard about the Varela Project petition? It's to exploit a loophole in our Constitution so we can have really free elections that are open to more than one party. More than 11,000 people have signed it, including me. And there's an underground film circulating in Havana, showing Castro at a party, drinking Dom Perignon champagne, eating Beluga caviar, living the good life—I mean, he's supposed to be just like the rest of us!"

"Don't you think things will improve after Castro is gone?"

"It's going to be a mess: Everyone will be jockeying for power. You know, I have asked other clients for help before. One guy ran an import company, and I asked him if I could stow away on his boat. He told me he would get into too much trouble. But I know that if I can just get out, I will make it. Even if I am dropped in the middle of Siberia, I will figure out a way to survive.

"Here is my plan: I will save enough money to fly to the Dominican Republic or Puerto Rico. It will take about a year to do all the paperwork, to get the exit visa. I will say I'm going to develop tourism there. I will need about 2,000 dollars. Then, once I am there, someone can buy me a ticket and sponsor me to come to America. Eventually I will get a green card and bring over my family."

"Teseo, you might not like the U.S. We have a lot of crime, for example, and there are other negative things about America." I said this to play the Devil's Advocate, to vet him, to see if he was really serious.

"I know all that! But I am thirty-eight years old, and I don't want to be my father's age and riding a bicycle!" He glared at me and took an angry drag on his *popular* cigarette. "The Cuban government tells you they take care of the people, but it is not true. Did you know that there is really a class system now in Cuba? They try to deny it, but look: They are now forbidding parties for school kids that the parents organize. You know why? Because some parents can provide more food and toys than others, and they want us all to be equal. And all the parents feel sorry for the teacher—she has been wearing the same dress for years—and we talk about pitching in to contribute some money to her, but then we say to ourselves, 'Why should we? The government is supposed to provide for her.' More and more teachers are quitting and going into tourism just to make some money. The kids are now being taught by putting them in front of computers and ignoring them."

As Teseo went on, I flashed on my own family history. My Jewish grandparents escaped from Russia during the pogroms at the beginning of the century and started over again in America. A charitable donor paid their way and gave them the chance to have a future. Could I not offer Teseo the same help? If anyone had the intelligence, motivation, and ambition to make it outside Cuba, it was Teseo.

"Teseo," I said, "I will help you get out." He looked sideways at me, squinting and exhaling smoke while maintaining eye contact. I sensed his doubt: *I've heard it all before. This is just another empty promise.* We left the conversation at that. We still had a long way to go on the tour and plenty of time to talk.

"I have a special treat for you," Steve announced to us one evening. We were in Cienfuegos now, on the southern coast. "We are going for a sunset cruise." As we boarded the boat, a beautiful catamaran, Teseo clarified something. "I'm only allowed on board because we're on the south side of the island and the captain trusts me. Cubans are not allowed to own private boats or to fish; this is why you see no boats on the waterfront in Havana." But then, as if remembering something, he suddenly stood up straight and made a public declaration in a serious tone of voice. "Don't get me wrong: I love my country and my job. I could never leave." He then broke into a big smile, a non-verbal sign of deception. "Also," he continued, "Cubans aren't allowed to eat lobster; it's served only to the tourists." But surprise, surprise, the two government workers on the boat have set up well-concealed lobster traps somewhere out on the water. We motored over; they retrieved their catch, and we had an opportunity to eat fresh lobster for dinner. We were advised to "tip" them five dollars a plate, almost half-a-month's salary for a Cuban and a bargain for us.

Earlier, in our hotel, Teseo hadn't been allowed to join us in the bar. Now I asked him, "Teseo, what would happen if we, as a group, insisted on having you join us in the bar?"

He laughed. "They would just give me a hard time when you leave. I would get the worst hotel room, the worst coffee, and they would accuse me of being a trouble-maker." Well, it didn't hurt to ask.

We had been warned to always keep an eye on our backpacks and personal possessions. On our last day in the countryside, at Topes de Collantes, we went on a hike to a waterfall, up a rocky trail. Steve and Tom, a group member, ran ahead of us because they knew there was a swimming hole at the end of the trail, and they wanted to jump in. As we arrived we saw them running to meet us, with some bad news.

"We left our packs on the shore, and as soon as we were in the water, two guys came down the hill and grabbed them. We tried to chase them, but they got away." Steve and Tom stood there half-naked, without shoes.

Steve was distraught. "I had everything in there—my passport, my money, even my tips from my guiding in Bolivia and Peru—about 5,000 dollars in cash."

We loaned them our shoes, and they ran up the hill to see if they could find anything, but they returned empty-handed. Sitting on the ground, Steve was then swarmed by fire ants, and one even got into his eye. Steve and those of us who had waited with him made our way back up the path to the ranger station at the head of the trail. When we explained what happened, the park ranger apologized profusely. Soon the police showed up and arrested two young men who had been loitering in the area. They were taken to the station but wouldn't confess. Teseo said, trying to keep a straight face, "Unfortunately we don't have the right to torture them."

Later we heard that another two teenagers had been found, and their parents, high military officials, were handling it rather than turning them over to the cops. The kids hid the backpacks somewhere in the woods, and dogs were supposedly being brought in to search. Meanwhile, the group had to move on, shaken by this misadventure. Tom said, "As soon as we leave, the whole thing will be forgotten, and they'll probably split the take."

Arriving back in Havana, we went immediately to the U.S. Special Interests Section to get a new passport for Tom. The main police station was also there. We passed the plaza where the statue to Elián González was located and got off the bus to photograph it. "Don't point your cameras at the soldiers," Teseo cautioned. The uniformed soldiers who guarded the plaza stood with their legs apart and their hands behind their backs, an impenetrable phalanx. Their berets gave them panache, and the men looked watchful but bored. When I got back on the bus and checked them out from the safety of the window, one of them smiled at me and puckered his lips in a kiss, making me laugh. I found Cuban men to be wonderfully flirtatious. One of the women on our trip, who was seventy-five but looked fifty, had received several marriage proposals. Steve also received the attentions of a young woman with a child. He was already married, and naturally wary: "They would love to find a way out of here."

Back in our hotel, the group was getting restless. Steve and Teseo, consumed with passport and money issues, did not have time to attend to the rest of us, and Teseo was trying to herd us back on the bus to go to a meeting of a neighborhood Committee for the Defense of the Revolution, the watch-dog group that exists on every block in order to keep an eye on the population. Marlene decided to stay back. She and I started talking in the room, and I suddenly looked at my watch and realized I was going to be late. Running into the lobby, I saw Steve standing there, barefoot. "Hurry," he urged. "The bus is just leaving." But as I ran down the street after it, Don Juan Carlos apparently didn't see me and hit the gas. The bus sped away, leaving me in a wake of exhaust fumes, yelling and waving my arms.

The next day I got the report, and it was clear I didn't miss much. Someone captured the event on video and played it back for me. One of the *cederistas* had jumped in front of the camera and monopolized it with a canned speech. But Teseo told me another version. "Some guy came in drunk and started yelling, 'This whole thing is bullshit!' and they had to take him away. I wonder what happened to him."

On our last day in Havana, we were scheduled to take a tour of the Partagás cigar factory. But before we got off the bus, Steve had something to tell us.

"If you are interested in buying cigars at a good price, this is the place to do it." He jumped off the bus and Teseo immediately jumped back on.

"Don't even think about buying cigars inside," he advised (with a smile). It's illegal, so don't bargain on the sly." We got it. They had obviously rehearsed this routine before.

Inside the cigar factory, the air was dense with the smell of tobacco, to the point that, after a few minutes, I could barely breathe. A thin layer of powdery tobacco covered every horizontal surface. I made the mistake of sitting down for a minute to rest, and my beige pants were now brown.

On the stage a burly *mulato*, with a large stogy hanging from his mouth, was reading something into a microphone. This was the official reader, carrying on a tradition that goes back to the time of independence from Spain. The reader started with the newspaper and read for about thirty minutes at a time throughout the day to provide entertainment for the workers, who sat side-by-side at their stations, engaged in various activities that would turn tobacco leaves into cigars. The workers could request something for him to read, such as a novel. His job was considered prestigious; he was apparently paid a higher salary than the other workers.

We walked to each station along the assembly line, as the factory guide explained what we were seeing. "Tobacco leaves have four main characteristics and are sorted accordingly for combustion ability, aroma, strength, and binding effect. Working in the factory is a good job for a Cuban. They have a daily quota to meet, and they can earn a bonus by exceeding the quota."

And if they weren't already addicted to tobacco, they soon would be. To us tourists, educated about the dangers of tobacco use, it was a shock to see many of the workers happily puffing away on cigarettes as they worked. "Do you have a lot of lung cancer in Cuba?" I inquired.

"We don't have any lung cancer here," our guide retorted, insulted that I would even consider asking such a question.

Mike, one of the men in our group, had indicated a desire to buy cigars under the table. When we reached the quality control station at the end of the tour, a cigar-tester was categorizing cigars by taking a puff on each one. A subtle sign passed between him and our guide—I'm not sure if it was a word or a wink—and the tester got up from the table and moved aside, while the guide moved in and deftly picked up a handful of cigars. It was arranged in advance that Mike would pay him downstairs. This all happened quite seamlessly and went past me, until Mike explained it to me later.

"I'm surprised you didn't want to buy any yourself," Steve laughed. "It seems like your kind of thing." He apparently had my number, but I was not interested in bringing back cigars, even legal ones.

Rum was a different story. I loved the Cuban rum, especially the *añejo*, the dark, aged kind. And we were going to a rum factory, where the antiquated machinery appeared to be something out of a cartoon. At the end of the tour we were escorted into a shop that sold both rum and coffee. There was a bar in one corner, and the bartender offered us a special drink: cappuccino flambé, for only a couple of dollars. It was a delicious concoction of strong coffee and a shot of rum, with hot milk. Now this was something I wouldn't normally drink at 10:30 a.m., but who could resist? This was smart marketing, for soon we were all very relaxed, and we happily parted with some more of our CUCs in the boutique.

It was our last day in Cuba and we were having our farewell dinner at the hotel. I went down to the lobby early hoping to find Teseo to show him the album of colonial stamps I had bought from a vendor at the flea market. I also had a package of clothing and toys for his children, and we had a few minutes to talk privately before the rest of the group arrived. While we were waiting to enter the restaurant, we received another visitor from Global Exchange to see how we enjoyed our trip. This time it was Estelle, all dressed up. We didn't have much time to chat before dinner, but she confirmed what we had heard. "The rumor is that Castro is sick. He hasn't been seen on TV lately."

Teseo, Juan Carlos, and Steve were in attendance at dinner. It was the last time we would all be together as a group and the last opportunity they would have to get tips. Speeches were made; I embarrassed myself and Teseo by standing up and thanking him personally, something that would be appreciated in America but probably brought unwanted attention in Cuba. I even made a stupid joke about seeing Fidel in the agro market. I still did not know enough to keep my mouth shut.

Finally it was time to say farewell to my Cuban brother. Teseo looked sad. "When are you coming back?"

"I'm not sure. Perhaps the next time I see you it will be in a free country."

"We will have to tug," he said, smiling at me and pulling on an imaginary rope with both hands.

"Stay strong."

"I am!" His eyes lit up.

I made sure Teseo had my email and home addresses, and all my phone numbers. I handed him my card. On it I wrote, "Keep the faith." This was another Cuban joke: The word "faith" in Spanish is *fe*. Teseo told me the initials meant "family in the exterior," the hope of getting out. I, myself, had faith that if we put our heads together we could figure out the necessary steps to get him off the island.

I returned home and fell into my usual routine, but something had changed for me psychologically. Cuba had touched me, again, and Teseo stayed on my mind. Every day I remembered my commitment to get him out of Cuba. I also knew that taking on this challenge wasn't necessarily rational, and I had no idea what it would involve. It just felt like the right thing to do. I no longer wanted to save the world, but perhaps I could change the destiny of one Cuban family.

I expected to hear any day from Teseo, imagining that he, too, remembered our talks, and that we were connected by our clandestine plan. I now saw my desire to help him as an inevitable evolution of my political thinking on Cuba, an act that might atone for my youthful, blind support of the Revolution.

A year went by, and I clung to my pledge, but I never heard from Teseo, not one word.

V

Cursed

In the month of October, the climate in Cuba was quite agreeable, not too hot, not too humid. The light was just bright enough to let you know you were in the tropics. At night it was breezy, requiring a jacket or sweater. It would have been lovely if it weren't for the air-conditioning, which apparently had only two settings in Cuba—off and freezing. It was stifling outside, but our tour bus and the buildings we entered appeared to be sub-zero, requiring that we take a jacket everywhere. The impossibility of adjusting quickly to these rapid temperature extremes made most of us sick by the end of the trip.

It was 2004, and I was back on Planet Cuba, only ninety miles from U.S. soil, and the flight was short, but I felt like I was traveling light-years in time and space, crossing the galaxy to get there. This time I managed to join a Global Exchange delegation investigating environmental issues, organic agriculture, and sustainable energy. The group was a conglomeration of races and ages from all over the U.S., interesting people I wouldn't normally get to meet. I was going back to the island in search of my Cuban brother, Teseo; I needed a legal way to get there, and this was it.

Flying into Havana from Cancun, I noticed there weren't as many lights below as last year. The price of oil was now up to $54/barrel, and large swaths of ground were blacked out. We arrived at the airport at the same time as hundreds of other travelers. The baggage-claim area was chaotic; we had to wait over an hour for our baggage to arrive, until we figured out we were standing at the wrong carousel. When we finally emerged with our suitcases, our Global Exchange contacts, Michele and Leonel, were waiting for us. Even with the baggage debacle, we weren't the last to arrive. Seven people were still coming in from Ohio and New York to make a film on organic urban agriculture in Cuba.

On the bus into Havana, Leonel, our Cuban guide for the first two days, launched into an angry and defensive lecture. "You probably don't think so, but there really IS democracy in Cuba," he insisted. As far as I can tell, no one brought up the subject, but he continued to scold us. He leaned forward, raised his voice, and scowled menacingly as he explained to us dumb Americans, "Cubans can choose delegates to the National Assembly at the neighborhood level, and anyone can be nominated. This is even MORE democratic than the democracy you have in the U.S.!"

Teseo had explained to me how the Cuban system worked. "There are, indeed, elections on the municipal level, but the candidates have to belong to one of the government-controlled organizations, such as the Federation of Cuban Women, or the Workers Union, which doesn't allow workers to negotiate wages or go on strike. Then, as you go up the ladder to regional elections, things are more controlled, until you get to the National Assembly, Cuba's excuse for a legislature. The National Assembly, the legislature, meets twice a year and rubber-stamps what the Council of Ministers decides. The Council decides what the dictator, the executive branch, tells them to decide. There is no separation of powers. In effect, Castro controls all branches of government—executive, legislative, and judicial."

Listening to Leonel, I had a hard time keeping a straight face, especially as he escalated his rhetoric. "All our leaders are chosen democratically, even the President of the country!" I actually had to hide behind the seat in front of me so he couldn't see me laughing, and I said, to no one in particular, *Yeah, and if you believe that, I have a bridge in San Francisco I'd like to sell you.*

Leonel ended with "The real reason Bush doesn't want Americans coming to Cuba is because he's afraid they will want communism in the U.S.!" *Yeah, right; that must be the reason.* At least he admitted it was communism, not socialism.

When I told Teseo about Leonel's rant later, we both laughed hysterically. It wasn't too hard to track Teseo down. I had emailed his tour company in Havana before leaving home, and they gave me his personal email. I was nervous about how he might react to hearing from me after all this time—he might not even remember me—but he seemed pleased when I wrote him I was coming back to Havana. "Call me at home the minute you get settled in the hotel," he replied, and I did. "Hey! It's nice to hear your voice. Listen, I just got back from a very long trip. I spent a week guiding a group of all different nationalities: Irish, Australian, English, and Danish, an explosive mix. They fought with each other the whole time. I'm exhausted. I need to go to bed. Call me tomorrow morning, and we'll figure out when we can get together. Big hug."

The next morning I woke him up. "Hmm. Hello," he mumbled, half asleep.

"I know you are not a morning person," I said and we laughed, remembering how I learned not to talk to him at breakfast until he had downed at least two *cafecitos*. I pictured him now sitting slumped over, with a cigarette in his hand, eyes barely open, looking miserable.

"But this is a good phone call," he added. We agreed to meet in the hotel lobby after dinner.

His face lit up when we finally saw each other. And holding his hand was Natasha, his wife. I was not expecting her. She was shorter than Teseo, and younger. She had long, black, curly hair, intelligent brown eyes, and a beautiful smile. I felt awkward. Was she looking at me with suspicion? Teseo proudly pointed to her belly, "Look!" Natasha was visibly pregnant with their second child.

Oh, I thought. *He won't be interested in getting out of Cuba now. I better not even bring up the subject. No wonder he never contacted me.*

How little I understood the Cuban reality.

"Let's have a drink and talk," I suggested. We sat in the lobby restaurant, and Teseo ordered a beer; Natasha requested lemonade, and I had my usual bottle of water.

"Tourism is really slow right now," Teseo began. "The Cuban government is consolidating tour companies under the slogan *Less is*

More, which really means that people are getting laid off. I even had two months without work where my boss just sent me home, without pay of course." Teseo punctuated this with a chuckle of resignation and an exhalation of cigarette smoke.

"I see you haven't lost your sense of humor," I noted.

"That's all we have! Everyone here is waiting for the American election; they think that Kerry will win and that tourism will pick up. Things are especially tough in the countryside, with all the power blackouts. The electricity that is generated goes mainly to the capital." I was suddenly aware of all the bright lights blazing in the hotel.

"Is this the fault of the *bloqueo*?" I asked. Teseo scoffed. "Trade with the U.S. continues to go on, and this is obvious to everyone. For example, the Cuban government imports cooking oil from Kansas that comes in a bottle with an American flag on the label. Even though it's more expensive, everyone wants it because it's so good. The same thing with the chicken that is imported from the U.S.; the Cubans prefer it."

As for the new U.S. restrictions that allowed Cuban-Americans to visit Cuba only once every three years, he told me they aren't really being enforced. "Some Cuban-Americans already had purchased tickets when the restrictions on travel were announced. Some were already in Cuba. The U.S. tried to send empty planes to get them back before the new deadline, but the airlines secretly sold tickets to fill the seats on the way over. The U.S. government discovered this and made them cancel the flights. You can imagine the scene at the Miami airport with all the Cuban-Americans screaming that they wanted their money back; you know how Cubans are!" Teseo imitated a lot of pushing and swearing. "Anyway," he continued, "I want to stop touring. I'm getting tired."

"I've cut down at the office also," said Natasha. "I felt too guilty because my son was saying *All the other mommies stay home*. So I go into the office only a couple of days a week. I'm sorry I couldn't bring him to meet you, but we wouldn't be able to talk with him here."

I figured there would be no more talk about getting Teseo out of Cuba. But I did want to stay involved with them and help. At one point in our conversation, the words just slipped out of my mouth:

"I'll be your family in the exterior." Was I insane? They must have wondered.

Rachel, our Global Exchange leader, met us the next day. She carried her six-month old daughter, dressed in a Ché T-shirt, who quickly became the mascot of the group. Rachel, sleep-deprived as most mothers are, was a bit disorganized. Naturally most of her attention was reserved for her child, and she resented any of our questions or demands. "I am not a tour guide," she snapped. "You are going to have to figure things out for yourself."

I asked Rachel if she lived in Havana. "I live in Los Angeles, but the baby's father is Cuban. Right now he's in Switzerland, making money by playing guitar. I'm staying with his family in Havana." Later in the trip, after a *mojito* or two, Rachel expressed her anger and sense of abandonment. "The baby's father shows no interest in returning to Cuba, or to me and our child. I keep telling him, 'You've never even seen your daughter!'" Probably he felt better being off the island, where he could make money to send to his family, but that was something an American woman wouldn't necessarily understand.

Rachel informed us that the group of filmmakers joined our tour at the last minute. "They'll fit right in and won't be disruptive to the group," she assured us. The title of the film they were shooting on this trip was *How Cuba Survived Peak Oil*. Their thesis was that we in the First World have reached the point where we're running out of oil, and we would do well to look to Cuba's experience during the Special Period to see how it survived the collapse of the Soviet Union in the 1990s, and the subsequent withdrawal of Soviet aid. Cuba, according to them, was a "model for what will take place in the rest of the world, as we learn how to deal with energy adversity."

The film-makers seemed sincere, and they were aware of the contradictions in the premise that Cuba was working hard on environmental issues—the air pollution from the buses and trucks, the factories belching out smoke, and the tourist hotels in Old Havana ablaze with lights while other parts of the country were blacked out. We did not even have those little cards in the bathrooms that asked guests to use our towels more than once and turn off the lights when we left the room. Did Cuba really have anything to teach us about energy conservation?

Teseo and I were having dinner in Le Chansonnier, a *paladar*, a private restaurant limited to twelve people. A friend from the group, Marie, was with us, flirting a bit with Teseo, and we were making idle conversation, when suddenly Teseo dropped a bomb. "Did you know that all Cubans are born with a stamp on their butt?" We looked at him like, *Huh? What are you talking about?* "It says CURSED!" He took a dramatic drag on his cigarette, expelling the smoke from one side of his mouth, turning his face away so he wouldn't make me cough and launch into my usual rant about his tobacco addiction.

"Did you know that Natasha and I are now officially divorced? That way I will be able to marry someone else, from the exterior. It's a way to get an exit permit, the Freedom Card, so I can leave. Don't look so shocked; this is a common strategy. A lot of couples do this. You pay an attorney for a legal divorce, and then you pay to arrange a fake marriage to a foreigner. You get out of the country; later, you get a divorce and send for your real wife. It's strictly business; it's the only way to make some money for your family. Natasha supports this decision. She wants me to get out now, but I want to wait for four years, so I can help her with the new baby. I just hope Castro holds on for that long. My main fear is that things will be even more of a mess when he dies."

I'm sat in stunned silence, and Marie was all ears. "You know the joke, don't you?" Teseo continued. "Someone gives Castro a Galapagos tortoise for a gift and tells him that they live to be 400 years old. Castro thinks for a minute, shakes his head, and says *That's the trouble with pets, you get attached to them and then they die.* The Old Guy has been on television for three days now talking about the electricity problem, because everyone is angry about the blackouts. And he doesn't make any sense. He's really getting senile."

Finally I could respond. "So where would you go if you leave?"

"Anywhere! I could jump on a boat to Haiti. It's pretty close, and no one else wants to go there. And I speak French. I also have a friend in Sweden."

I finally got it. The fact that Teseo and Natasha had another child on the way made him even more determined to leave the island. He wanted to do what good husbands and fathers do, give his children opportunities that he never had.

"There is no future in Cuba," he said, matter-of-factly. "No future." He lowered his head, took another contemplative pull of tobacco, and suddenly screamed I HAVE TO GET OUT OF HERE!

"¡*Cálmate, chico*! Calm down!" I said, worried, patting his arm. You never knew who was listening, and I had picked up the habit in Cuba of being careful in public. No one in the restaurant seemed to notice Teseo's outburst; at least, no one looked our way. Or maybe this kind of explosion was common, and people knew to avert their eyes.

The producer of the film was looking for someone to act as a paid interpreter for the crew on their next trip to Cuba, and they wanted more interviews with Cubans about the Special Period. I suggested Teseo for both these things, and we set up a meeting for later that night. We met in the lobby after dinner, and Teseo hailed a pedicab to pedal us to the Golden Phoenix restaurant in Chinatown. The seat in the cab had room for only two adults, so Teseo positioned himself on my lap. I gingerly put my hands on his back to balance him. He was so thin I could feel his ribs through his shirt.

Havana's version of Chinatown was about a block long, with many restaurants and an equal number of child-beggars harassing the tourists. There were, in fact, a small percentage of Chinese in the Cuban population. Often when someone had Chinese-looking features, they were called *chino*, as an affectionate nickname. Cubans also good-naturedly called each other *negro, mulato, gordo* (fatty), *flaco* (skinny), and other adjectives that we might consider insulting rather than endearing.

The restaurant was crowded and noisy, good cover for conversation, and we climbed a couple flights of stairs to be seated. Teseo agreed to help the producer with her research on the Special Period. He was chain-smoking as usual, and at one point Faith couldn't take it anymore and whispered to me, "I have to leave; I'm really not feeling well. I shouldn't have had that beer."

Teseo found this behavior strange. "A Cuban wouldn't have come out in the first place if he's not feeling well."

"We Americans," I explained, "have a limited amount of time here, and we don't allow being sick to get in our way." But things got a little more relaxed between us once the producer departed. Teseo and I could talk about our plans more openly.

"I actually got Swedish papers before my son was born. Natasha was angry because I wouldn't leave then. She is very strong."

I mentioned to Teseo earlier that there was no milk in the hotel at breakfast. "Someone probably ripped it off and took it home," I said knowingly.

"Actually, the guy with the key to the milk probably didn't turn up. Don't you know the joke about the difference between the capitalist Hell and the socialist Hell? A Cuban goes to Hell and the Devil gives him a choice between a capitalist Hell and a socialist Hell. The Devil lets him peek through a keyhole to see both, so he can make a decision. In the capitalist Hell there is someone in a pot of boiling water and another person stirring the pot. It's exactly the same in the socialist Hell. *What's the difference?* the guy asks. *It looks exactly the same to me. Well,* explains the Devil, *that's because it's Monday. In the capitalist Hell it's like this all week, but in the socialist Hell, the guy who builds the fire doesn't show up on Tuesday, the guy who pours water in the pot doesn't show up on Wednesday, and the guy who stirs the pot doesn't show up on Thursday.*

When we stepped outside the restaurant, pedicab drivers surrounded us, clamoring to be chosen to bicycle us to our destination. They were yelling something I didn't understand. Teseo picked one of the drivers, explaining that he was saying, "*¡Con el negro!* Pick me, the Negro!"

Three minutes into the trip a cop appeared and signaled our driver to pull over. "Don't say anything," Teseo cautioned. "Pretend you're my girlfriend." As we got out of the cab, the cop checked the driver's permit and identity card. The driver looked at us apologetically, and I wanted to at least pay him something for the fare, but Teseo grabbed my arm and hissed, "Let's get out of here!"

It was hot and humid, a Saturday night, and the streets were full of people, mainly young Afro-Cuban men, milling around. We heard sirens and saw flashing lights; people began to run. I wanted to see what was happening. "No!" insisted Teseo. His face and body were tight with fear. I felt it emanating from him in waves. He pulled me down the street, nimbly navigating a construction zone, and when we were several blocks away, he began to breathe normally and let go of my arm. "When you see those flashing lights," he explained, "you run. My mother always told me to move out and get away when there are police around. Sometimes they will block off a whole area and round up everyone. Even if you are a good person, it can take hours at the police station to prove it."

As we walked back, Cuban men tried to talk to me, and Teseo warned them off. "They think I'm Spanish or something by the way I dress. I open my mouth, and they hear I'm Cuban." I haven't understood a word he said in Cuban slang, but whatever it was, it worked, and no one bothered me.

At the entrance to the hotel, it was time to part. I hated these good-byes with Teseo and usually tried to soften my sadness at leaving him by chiding him some more about his smoking. He and I hugged and I quickly walked away, without looking back.

VI

The Battle of Ideas

My next trip to Cuba was in December 2004, to research education in Cuba. Our Global Exchange leader was a teacher, social worker, and student of Latin American history. I met up with Leslie again, the former *brigadista* who was on her seventeenth year in Cuba, working for Radio Havana and as an attorney for Global Exchange. Our Cuban guide was a former teacher who had switched to tourism in order to make more money, like so many other young Cubans.

Our first day we went to the Casa de Amistad, Friendship House, run by ICAP, the *Instituto Cubano de Amistad Con Los Pueblos*, the Cuban Institute of Friendship with the Peoples. Headquartered in Havana, they also had branches in other provinces in Cuba, and in Europe, Latin America, Asia, the Middle East, Africa, and North America. Their American counterpart is called the National Network on Cuba, set up to "develop activities to support Cuba, to end the blockade, do educational work, and foster ways of normalizing relations." Global Exchange, naturally, is part of the Network, as are Pastors for Peace, and the Venceremos Brigade. In other words, all these groups accepted and supported the Cuban government propaganda about all the good work the Cuban government was doing in Cuba and around the world. Any problems the regime experienced were the fault of the U.S. *bloqueo*.

"We are not a threat to the United States," the Cuban spokesman, Ulexi, began. "Cuba is developing its own social pride, through health care, sports, and education. Of course there are weak points that need improvement, but we Cubans want to do this in our own way. Forty years of the blockade and the economic war on Cuba makes things very difficult, but we distinguish the American people from the American government. We have shown that we have a capacity to resist the blockade."

Someone asked a question about the political dissidents who are in prison, couched in the context of "How large is the prison population?"

Ulexi had a stock answer: "There are no political prisoners. Most of the prisoners have been accused of burglary or drug possession. There is a small amount of drug dealing, compared to other countries." He also mentioned that "people are being paid to study and to enter any university program for free."

Another question: "Is there any possibility of friendship between Cuba and the Cuban exiles in Miami?"

"The majority of people leaving Cuba now are leaving for economic reasons. In early years it was the wealthy landowners who left for political reasons. These people are throwing stones all the time; we cannot throw flowers in return. But their children and grandchildren don't have the same hostility."

I asked a lawyer in our group. "When you are talking about a state-centralized economy and a political system that does not allow dissent or reward individual effort, is there a difference between an economic and a political reason to leave?"

"Seems to me," she replied, "that those who leave for economic reasons today are also casting a political vote with their feet."

When I got together again with Teseo, he announced, "I want you to go to the U.S. Interests Section. No, don't look nervous. It's very simple; they will let you in without any problem. You have your passport with you, right? I just want you to pick up any forms they might have about applying for a visa."

We ambled over to the Interests Section, and Teseo stopped halfway down the block and sat on a bench. "I'll wait here; you go ahead." He pointed me toward the entrance, where I waved my

American passport at the friendly Cuban guards. I got through security, much like at the airport, except without the long line, and they asked me to please leave my camera behind. Once inside, I was surprised at the number of Cubans who were in the waiting room. Perhaps they were among the visa applicants the U.S. promises to accept every year.

Being inside our "embassy" was like being in a different country. On the wall was a "wanted" poster for Assata Shakur (JoAnne Chesimard), showing her "disguises"—none of them like the suburban matron I saw waiting in the lobby of our hotel to contact someone from Global Exchange. There was also a Christmas tree with photos of the imprisoned journalists and librarians, with a star at the top that said "75," the number arrested in the last sweep. (Apparently there was also a "75" sign along the waterfront, because Natasha later told me she wondered what it meant when she drove along the Malecón.) I found the forms and instructions for the visa application process. The whole task took less than thirty minutes.

I returned to Teseo and gave him the information. "Well," he said, acting not really interested, "I wanted you to have the experience of going in there." We decided to go to the Jazz Café, where they had excellent food and better-than-usual service. "The waiters and waitresses aren't old enough to be cynical," Teseo said. Having a drink and watching the sunset were favorite activities here, for Cubans and tourists alike, and it was a good place to have a heart-to-heart.

Teseo told me about his family. His parents were divorced. "My father was not that involved with us when we were kids. He was sent to the Soviet Union; my mother kept him alive for my sister and me by showing us his photo and talking about him. I know Natasha will do the same thing for our kids when I leave."

As for his career in politics, "I resigned from the Foreign Ministry in 1995. I was working there as an analyst; my specialty was the U.S. Congress. I wrote twenty-five pages on what I thought needed to be changed in the office. For this, they sent me to a farm labor camp to be re-educated. They tried to set me up to go to prison. They accused me of stealing pigs, of leaving the grain out in the rain. I confronted them. When I came back I told my boss I wanted to resign. I said, 'I will not drive the boat, but I will help push it'.

After that I was expelled from the Communist Party. I probably could have had a good life, maybe even become a foreign diplomat. But I don't regret my decision."

Suddenly Teseo introduced a total non sequitur, launching into a story about a handsome mulatto tour guide he once worked with who was approached by an American woman in their group. She had a big drink in her hand and passed it to the guide, telling him, "This drink is called *orgasm.*

"Oh, that was subtle," I interjected, fearing where this anecdote was leading.

"The guy told me, *Help, I'm going to be ra-a-a-aped.*" Teseo imitated a panicked reaction, and we both laughed. He suddenly looked at me with great seriousness. "Why are you helping me?"

"I don't know; it just feels like the right thing to do, and I like the challenge. Also, I'm Jewish, and someone helped my grandparents get out of Eastern Europe during the *pogroms.* It seems natural to help someone else."

Teseo wasn't satisfied with this answer and leaned forward in a confrontive manner. "Have *you* ever thought about having sex with *me?*" It was an interrogation, not a seduction.

"Teseo," I explained to him (and to myself), "I feel a connection with you, here and here." I touched my head and heart. "I suppose I do love you."

"No!" His voice was louder, more pressing. "Really, have you ever thought about having *sex* with me?"

"Well, okay, maybe," I admitted, thinking, *You're a man, aren't you?* "But don't worry, there's no way it's going to happen. You're way too young, and I'd be embarrassed to have a guy your age see me naked." *He's probably not even circumcised*, it occurred to me. I didn't know whether Cubans circumcised their boy babies, but, after all, I *was* Jewish.

"Thank God!" Teseo said, leaning back, taking a drag on his cigarette, and invoking a deity that neither one of us believed in. And at that moment, I have to admit, I felt a little hurt and insulted that he hadn't even considered having sex with me.

On the way back to the hotel, a sad song came on the cab radio, and tears of relief suddenly sprung into my eyes. I knew Teseo and I had crossed some kind of barrier in our friendship and were now at a different, more trusting, stage.

"What is going on with education now in Cuba, and in Cuban society in general, is the Battle of Ideas. These new programs are going to be the key for the future. They were launched five years ago, and now it's clear what the government meant when they said *cultura general integral*—comprehensive knowledge of every possible issue. They want Cubans to be prepared to face globalization and still retain their values." We were listening to a lecture by Juan Jacomino, who was a linguist by profession. He worked in radio journalism, covering economic issues. "When the U.S. sneezes," he said, "Cuba prepares to get a cold. You are here at a very interesting time. Cuba has embarked on a number of programs dealing with social issues. We now have a Deputy President of the Cabinet for the Council of Ministers who will be in charge of investment in these new programs of the Revolution. The youth organizations are at the center of these new programs, and new teachers are being given crash courses for primary and secondary education. We are building new classrooms, and remodeling and expanding existing schools.

"We are also training art instructors. Cuba attaches a great deal of importance to culture. By defending its culture, Cuba is defending its sovereignty and values. Cuba is trying to preserve the true national cultural values. New social workers are being trained to identify problems; there are more than twenty of these programs.

"Cuba is trying to come out of a difficult economic period. The economy is now growing at a rate of eighteen to twenty percent per year, due to tourism." Someone questions this figure. "We count services in our GDP figures, including health care and education."

At his home, Teseo told me later that this Battle of Ideas was Castro's shorthand for "We're going to sugar-coat my outdated ideas about the Revolution and ram them down your throats. Don't even think about changing the system I installed, you ingrates. And we'll distort our economic statistics to prove that it all works. The problem is not the system I created; it's that you people are not revolutionary enough."

"They have this idea of 'integral' education," said Teseo. "What that really means is that teachers are required to teach more than one subject because so many are leaving. But the teachers weren't consulted about this, and it doesn't work."

"My sister is an example," added Natasha. "She couldn't take teaching any more and quit. She is now working in agriculture. Part of the problem is that they now have the kids sitting in front of computers all day. They're not really teaching, just babysitting the kids."

Natasha brought out the book her son was using to learn the alphabet. "I had this same book when I was a kid," she said. It was a Russian schoolbook adapted to Cuban culture. *F is for Fidel; I is for imperialismo*. There were lots of drawings of rifles and people in military uniforms defending the Fatherland from the Imperialist Enemy. "Look, the spelling lesson contains the letter *k*, which doesn't even exist in the Cuban alphabet!"

I wanted a copy of the book to bring home. It was shocking in a way, so Cold War, so retro. It said a lot about what little kids were taught in Cuba. Natasha did try to get me one, but it turned out to be impossible. "They don't sell them anywhere, and you probably wouldn't be allowed to take it out of the country."

Our afternoon meeting with ICAP was canceled because of mandatory military exercises, the *bastion*. The U.S. government pledged not to invade Cuba when the Soviet missiles were removed in 1962, but Castro needed a reason to keep the population geared up and on a war footing. Also, he was paranoid about the U.S. invasion of Iraq.

Teseo was called for the *bastion* but refused to go. "I have a pregnant wife and a mother with asthma at home," he told them. "I can't leave." The next day he was angry: "They took over my phone line, just to show me. Good thing we didn't have any emergencies."

By now we have come up with a new plan: Someone in Canada will write a letter of invitation. Teseo will then take it to the Canadian Embassy and apply for a temporary visa to visit his Canadian "friend" for a short visit. I know someone who will write this letter and provide the necessary documentation. If it works, it means Teseo would be leaving his family behind for five years. At last he has made a decision about what country he wants to enter.

We left Havana for Santa Clara the next morning, to visit the university and learn about the history of the region. The first lecturer gave us the usual government-generated statistics. "At the present time there are 12,000 students enrolled in a five-year University program; 8,000 are taking post-grad courses for their Masters or PhD. In addition, there are eighty different collaboration projects with international students from Africa, Europe, Canada, and Asia. They hope eventually to have classes from all disciplines available on the Internet."

After lunch we visited a school for art instructors, where they taught a four-year program covering art, music, dancing, acting, and creative writing. We were told there were fifteen schools for art instructors in the country. The students put on a performance for us, singing and dancing. Then came a visit to the newly formed social workers. A young woman explained that the Young Communist League ran a one-year program to form workers in "social communication, sociology, English, Spanish history, and cultural/social events. These social workers will continue at the University to earn their degrees. We provide them with an ideological tool that prepares them to have all the knowledge in their hands."

On the list of things addressed by the social workers was this: "They also do preventive work with children to keep them out of prison." This was our cue, unexpected and unintentional on the part of the Cubans, for us to ask pointed questions about the prison population in Cuba. The speaker made an astonishing declaration: "Prisons have become educational. The prisoners study, and there are programs where people can get a degree."

Was she thinking of South Africa during the time Nelson Mandela was in prison? A group member asked about the seventy-five dissident journalists and librarians who were serving time. The Afro-Cuban woman who was giving us the government line stammered and lost her place in the memorized text. An older white man, the real person in charge, materialized behind her and tapped her on the shoulder, a signal for her to stop talking and let him take over. It wasn't even subtle, and everyone in our group commented on it later. The man now explained to us, in an authoritarian voice, "These dissidents are in the employ of the Imperialists, the U.S. They don't really represent what Cubans think."

Before this lecture turned into a real argument, our event guide rushed in waving his hands. "We have to hurry and get on the bus, or we'll miss our next appointment." Was this arranged on the spur of the moment to shut us up, or was it part of a back-up plan, in case we Americans got out of hand? We all managed to board the bus and were whisked off to visit a foster home for children.

That night there was another CDR meeting, where we were given those little Cuban flags waved at mass demonstrations. The *cederistas* asked us to sit in chairs, while they remained standing in front of us rather nervously, as if waiting for someone to say something. They apparently didn't have a good script to follow. Eventually we all managed to converse; then it was time to go back to our hotel and have dinner.

But something happened at the meeting that made one woman in our group very upset. She was an outspoken African-American woman, probably around my age, who had been telling the Cubans how horrible things are for blacks in the U.S. and how discrimination is "institutionalized," as if all the civil rights legislation and the anti-discrimination laws in the U.S. were never passed. During the CDR meeting she went around asking the older Cubans to please take her chair, putting them in a very awkward position. She couldn't understand why they refused, and she was upset with the rest of us for not following her example of good manners.

"I was brought up to always offer my seat to an older person. And I thought it was just terrible that we all sat there while some of the older people were standing."

"But," I asked her, "aren't you just engaging in another kind of imperialism, telling them what to do? Obviously they wanted us to accept their hospitality and sit in those chairs, and they could have been in trouble if they obeyed you."

She and I went back and forth about this, with a few other people pitching in and supporting my interpretation, and finally I said, "Look, I just don't want you to be so upset!"

She laughed, "Oh, I'm always upset about something!" This broke the tension, and I could almost hear everyone breathe a sign a relief.

A very beautiful African-American woman in our group was having her own problems. Every time she entered the hotel, the guards at the door challenged her. "They think I'm a *jinetera*, a prostitute. Who says there's no racial discrimination here?" On a past trip, she hooked up with a cab driver in Havana and was spending as much time with him as she could. "He calls me his fiancée, and he even introduced me to his whole family. They email me all the time!" As for the romantic image of waves coming over the Malecón wall, "As we were driving along, a big wave hit the side of the cab, and I got drenched. That damned air-conditioning doesn't help. I have a terrific earache."

The next day we visited a community project in Condado. "Originally a shanty town," our Cuban spokesperson began, "the Cuban government sent in a construction brigade to repair homes and build new ones. The government supplied the materials and the money; the people in the community provided the labor force. Our objective was to change conditions in the community. Over fifteen years, 160 houses and fifteen other buildings have been built, including this library, where we are meeting. The Battle of Ideas, ideological preparation and instruction, is geared toward getting a general level of integrated culture. Now I will let Maritsa speak. She is the founder of this library, the *Biblioteca Popular Condado*, the First Library of the Battle of Ideas."

Maritza had the floor. She had done a good job of memorizing all the statistics. "This library was the first of its kind. It was built in 2001. There are 6,183 books in the library, with 2,247 titles. We have 1,366 people registered to borrow books. They also come to study and to carry out activities for people in the community of all ages. We have some commemorative event every month, like the birthday of José Martí, homage to Ché, Camilo Cienfuegos, the Young Pioneers, or the Young Communists. There are ten workers in the library, also computers and technicians, and we show documentaries on a television. Children come to the library to do their homework. Nine hundred people come to the library every month, mainly children and adolescents."

Question time. Here we go. "Is there government control over selection of books?"

"Yes, so that there's universal culture and knowledge. We have a compilation of books from all over the world."

"It's wonderful that you have so many books and that the library is open to everyone," a group member says, diplomatically. "I wonder if you have a book I have heard about. It's called *Waiting for Snow in Havana*, about the Peter Pan operation."

An expression of panic flitted across the librarian's face. Our Cuban guide, the one who whisked us away during the last bout of embarrassing questions, sprang into action.

"Yes, yes, we have it! Let me see if I can find it for you!" And he ran, literally, into the stacks and came back waving a book. "Here it is!"

We wanted to believe they had it, but it wasn't *Waiting for Snow in Havana*, written by Carlos Eire. It was an entirely different book, published in Cuba, giving the Cuban version of the airlift, which was, essentially, "The U.S. stole our children." In Cuba, children belong to the State, not to their parents.

Okay, we got the point. We were making our guide extremely nervous with our questions, and we didn't really want to get him into trouble. We knew he had to do what he'd been told to do, say what he'd been told to say, whether he believed it or not. For me, Teseo's bravery became even more unusual by contrast.

VII

Gone Booking

Back in Havana, I had a free day for "individual research." This was an opportunity to do something with Teseo, my best source of information on Cuba. He picked me up in his car, a 1956 English Ford with a Lada engine that he and Natasha called *La Princesa*, also referred to as *el cacharro*, the jalopy. *La Princesa* was a four-door, scuffed-up white box. The passenger-side door didn't work, so we immediately developed a routine. I stood outside and pulled on the handle while Teseo jiggled it and pushed from the inside. It was the same push-pull routine to get out, a special ritual, predictable and satisfying. The car's interior was somewhat tattered, although the steering wheel had a leather cover. There was no radio or air-conditioning, and the window on my side didn't roll down, so Teseo had to lean over and pry loose the fly window to create a draft. I felt like a real *habanera* riding in *La Princesa*.

Of course we weren't supposed to be hanging out together, and Teseo made sure to wear his official tour-guide uniform—a blue polo shirt, khakis, official name tag— just in case. He was a great driver, used to negotiating the chaotic traffic of Havana. He also knew what might interest me, and on this day he took me on a tour of the various neighborhoods of Havana so I could see the different types of housing.

We began by driving through the high-class areas, through Miramar and Siboney, where many of the upper elite of the Communist Party and the Armed Forces lived in huge mansions. Most of the properties had lush landscaping, with flowers and trees in bloom. Occasionally we came across overgrown lots with abandoned mansions, the remnants of families who fled the Revolution.

Nuevo Vedado, another area with smaller, Spanish-style houses and groomed front lawns, reminded me of suburban Los Angeles. "Do you know who lives here?" Teseo asked. "Lots of artists. They are the new middle class."

Scattered among more traditional housing were buildings that looked like monolithic blocks of cement. "These were built by the micro-brigades," Teseo explained. We were far away from the tourist area by now, and Teseo drove past a bridge. "Look at all these people sleeping underneath. Who says there are no homeless people in Cuba? They're internal immigrants from the countryside, illegals in Havana without government permission. Do you know what we call them? *palestinos*."

We drove through Bosque, using a road that bordered one of Castro's many compounds, where guards were posted at various entrance points. "This road is a shortcut. Look through those trees; that's Castro's main home."

"What if we got out and took a picture?"

"If you even stop the car for one second an armed policeman will appear out of nowhere." We didn't stop. In any case, the house was too far away to get a good photo.

Next was a *barrio* where Teseo pointed out young men walking in the street waving around pieces of metal and calling out "*plomero, plomero*" to passing cars. "Look, these guys are selling plumbing supplies, and this is where you go if you need them, not to a store." As we drove through these streets, people crossed aimlessly in front of the car. "They don't care whether they get run over," Teseo sneered. "Do you think they would actually fight back if the U.S. invaded?"

All of a sudden we were on a dirt road in an Afro-Cuban neighborhood, where families lived in tiny cardboard shacks with tin roofs, and barefoot children played in the open sewers. The road was full of *baches*, potholes, containing muddy water, and suddenly *La Princesa* got stuck in one of these potholes, and Teseo had to get out and push.

We seemed to be attracting a crowd. I shrunk into the car seat. I heard too many stories of tourists being mugged in similar situations. I never wore jewelry and always tried to look low-key in Cuba, but it was obvious that I was a *yuma*, a foreigner, easy prey. Indeed, crime was on the increase in Havana, crime against tourists in particular. One couple in our group was robbed from a pedicab while at a stop, assaulted by a pedestrian, who ripped a gold chain from her neck, probably a set-up, according to her husband. Another member of our group, a tall, pretty blonde woman, often walked around Old Havana alone, always wearing a flashy pearl necklace. I figured it was just a matter of time for her.

Quickly we were out of the hole and on our way. "You can take that panicked look off your face now!" laughed Teseo.

"Okay, enough of the tour. Now let's go booking!" Teseo loved books and couldn't get enough of them. We drove to a bookstore run out of someone's home, something he called an "independent library." On the front porch was one set of books, but then we were taken into a back room, where another set of books was for sale. I couldn't find anything I particularly wanted—most of the books in English dated from the 1950s—and Teseo was looking for a specific book that he couldn't find either. Teseo was not sure whether this library was authorized by the government, or whether the owner of the books was selling them illegally. Independent literature was a big issue in Cuba, and many works that were banned by the government circulated under the table. The new technology of CDs and flash drives made the dissemination of black-market literature a lot easier.

Teseo took me to his own neighborhood, Playa. A beautiful *caoba*, a mahogany tree, graced the street in front of his house, a one-story structure divided into two apartments, one for Teseo and his family, one for his mother. This was a common solution to the housing-shortage problem in Cuba, and Teseo prided himself on the fact that he did all the plans and construction himself. "The government owns the housing," he explained, "but they don't pay for any repairs. We have to take care of them ourselves. And building materials are expensive, plus it's almost impossible to get them without having access to convertible pesos." Naturally Teseo had a joke about all the government promises to increase housing construction:

"If there were no future tense in Spanish, Castro would be speechless."

Mom's side of the house was stuffed to the gills with books, piled everywhere, and artwork on the walls, some of it framed magazine photos; Teseo's side of the house also contained books and artwork, original paintings, wooden sculpture, and beautiful antique furniture. I was envious of their roomy kitchen, with space for a table and chairs. "The kitchen is the heart of the home," he said.

There was a surreptitious knock at the door, and a woman quickly and quietly entered with a bag of powdered milk, which she was selling on the black market. Milk in the ration stores was not given to anyone over age seven, but it was available in the "dollar" stores at a very high price. I had already been conned into buying a bag of milk for a hustler who wanted it for his "baby," and this guy was probably doing the same thing as this woman. The transaction completed, she moved on to the next buyer.

Teseo smiled. "You know the Cuban joke, don't you? We have three basic rights here: the right to free education, the right to free health care, and the right to steal from the state."

When Natasha arrived we all cooked dinner together. Their stove was not working, so Natasha pulled a two-burner gizmo out of the cupboard and placed it on top of the stove so we could boil water for pasta. She produced some beautiful tomatoes, which she found at the farmers' market, and we chopped them up for sauce.

Dinner finished and the dishes done, we adjourned to the living room. Their son finished his homework and wanted me to sit with him on the living room couch and watch cartoons on the DVD player. Mom came over to visit from her side of the house but soon excused herself to watch a favorite soap opera on television.

The orange tabby cat, Leonardo, jumped into my lap and settled in, accepting me. "I wish you could stay with us," said Teseo. "Then you wouldn't have to stay in a hotel." It was a nice thought, but impossible. Cubans weren't supposed to socialize with foreigners; it was bad enough that I was hanging out with them at home.

VIII

Illegal Messaging

Teseo was able to get an illegal Internet connection, buying a password from a government official, so we were able to continue our discussions when I was not in Cuba. Occasionally we could even chat online in real time. Teseo's connection was programmed to go off periodically, so Cuban State Security could not detect it. What follows are excerpts from our conversations, which I saved verbatim.

During this time the Cuban government de-dollarized the economy and required Cubans to turn in their American dollars. Only Cuban convertibles and Cuban pesos could now be used in Cuba, and foreigners would have to change their currency into Cuban convertibles. The original deadline for this was November 8, 2004; however, as long lines formed and the supply of convertibles proved to be inadequate, the deadline had to be extended. The government was apparently caught off guard by the amount of dollars circulating in the economy. After a certain date, there would be a ten percent penalty to change dollars. Euros and Canadian dollars would now be the foreign currency of choice.

> _November 4, 2004:_ Natasha and I want more than ever to plan our escape. Castro has de-dollarized the economy. We expect more restrictions to follow. The future here is darker than ever. Rumors say that

there are more changes to come and more measures from the government to restrict our everyday lives. Cubans are cautious about changing dollars. A French friend is coming, and I will talk with him about going to France, as a first step. I am now considering France or Canada as the best plan. I'll keep you informed.

November 6, 2004: I haven't been in line yet to change money, and I think I won't. Remember I told you once that I still have my sources from friends I used to have at the university? Now some of them are part of the establishment. They have found a way to survive and navigate through all the bureaucracy, with profit and privileges. One of them is working at the Cuban Central Bank, and I asked him about future monetary issues. You're not going to believe this! The answer was "It's uncertain." He sounded so disappointed and concerned that I don't think he was hiding something. So people are changing their money, but there is no way to know how much. The government postponed the deadline for another week. This makes me wonder, and I don't trust the system at all. I'm not going to change our money into funny, worthless, Monopoly paper. All among our colleagues, we've been discussing this, and the general consensus is to keep the dollars in a safe, secret hole and see what happens. We hope our tips will come in convertible pesos from now on.

This is what I see: After ten long years of dollarization, some Cubans have become richer. Some have done better working in tourism, in services, and especially in foreign trade and affairs. Corruption at all levels is the first thing that comes to mind whenever you dig a little bit into how this society functions. The higher the level, the bigger the corruption.

It is also known that there is a tax war against small, private businesses (like restaurants). This society is such a disaster that the simplest private initiative is easily more competitive than the biggest government enterprise. So these private businesses have been doing well. Don't forget the farmers, who handle tons of money. Remember the campesino we visited in Viñales? That guy makes 60,000 pesos a year, only in tobacco, and some other money from small cultures he's got on the farm. I won't give details of the funny business he may make with a little portion of the tobacco that doesn't really go through the official system, which ends up on Havana streets as "inexpensive" black-market cigars.

The government ended up painting itself into a corner. How could it cut down on this growing underground Cuban business, all these "secret" black, competitive markets? How do they stop the high officials using their connections and their dollars to control economic activities? Then comes the big news: We have to stop using the dollar in the national territory. A dollar will cost ten percent more in Cuban convertible pesos. Amazing! But if you put your money in a bank before November 8, you will have the right to take it out any time, in dollars. This is a clear message to me: They need our dollars. If you don't hand them over, you will have less for every dollar you hide.

In the street, people understand this, and the general thinking is, Let's change some money for everyday life but keep the biggest part safe. A dollar is a dollar, Cubans say, and it will be like that, longer than Fidel will live. Some are buying gold, or art, which is not a bad idea, but most people think the final result is that the dollar will cost much more than 1.10 convertibles, because, as usual, the government won't sell dollars after this, and people who need them will pay anything to get them, because

Cubans don't much trust the convertibles. All the traditional transactions will still be in dollars: a house, a car, a computer, or anything. In months the black market will establish the top, and any business reaching more than a certain amount of convertibles will have to be done in dollars. If a transaction is under 1,000 dollars, people will accept convertibles, but a classic car, valued at 8,000 or 10,000, won't be sold unless you pay in dollars.

There is a joke now: Two friends meet in the street. "Hey, have you changed yet?" "Not yet," says the other. "I'm waiting." "Waiting for what?" asks the friend. The guy takes a look around and whispers, "I'm waiting for the next fall."

So, baby, this is Cuba. You know me and you know how much I love this country. But here is a fact: Whenever I see my mother, who turned sixty-one this year, I feel really bad. She was sixteen when the Revolution came. Now she's sixty-one, and she's got a fucking pension of 142 Cuban pesos. She depends on me even to buy toilet paper. She doesn't really own her house; she doesn't even have a 100-dollar bank account. She's got nothing at all. She's like a lamb, poor woman, and she hides all her frustration because she wants us to keep going, but I don't want to end that way. So I will keep my money safe, and I will find a way out for my own family.

November 11, 2004: This is really amazing. It's 10:00 o'clock in the morning, and here at home we've been talking for two hours about the situation and what could happen in the near future. There is a general feeling that the funny money won't last long, maybe as long as Mr. F. does. Then, as we say in Cuba,"A new rooster will crow."

This country is a mess, a total mess. The government hasn't collected as much as they thought. Cubans don't want to get rid of their dollars (they're not that stupid), so look at this: To encourage the changing process, the government is sending "people" to the banks to "change" 20,000, 30,000, and 50,000 dollars. You may agree with me that no normal person would make such a stupid move, not just in Cuba, but anywhere in this world. The last thing that anyone who has thousands of dollars would buy is *chavitos*, as we call the convertibles, so how come a guy from the "people" is going to change 20,000 U.S. dollars? I don't buy it, and no Cuban will, not even if José Martí comes out of his grave and tells me so. Rumors say that already people are paying thirty-three Cuban pesos for one dollar in the streets.

You asked about getting married to foreigners. This has been one of the biggest practices in Cuba for the past ten years. Thousands of Cubans are leaving that way. The problem with getting married to an American is that there is no guarantee that after the marriage one would get permission to live in the U.S. It could take years for the U.S. Immigration Service to approve the application. And American women are very skeptical about getting married to a poor Cuban, because getting divorced could mean paying a lot of money. I don't blame them at all. It is much easier for other nationalities; for instance, a Mexican, or any Central American. If I could have found a Central American woman to get married to, I would have left in a blink. Remember this, Regina: The big priority here is TO GET OUT. If I get a work permit in Siberia, I will take it, because once you're out, the chance to make decisions gets a thousand times bigger. And with money, everything works. That's another reality, like it or not. There is something I am sure of: If I find a safe way to get out, even to Antarctica, I will hit the ball and survive. There is a Cuban saying: "In the country of the blind, the one-eyed man is king."

A Caribbean island is also a choice. It's easy and pretty inexpensive to go there by plane. If you get to American land, you have the right to stay, even if you don't have relatives. If you have an American friend who claims the "Cuban right to stay" for you and pays the fees, you're in. The Immigration officials verify that you are who you say you are, and they just make the American friend sign something saying he or she will be in charge of you until the paperwork is done. You probably don't know that there is direct communication between the U.S. Coast Guard and the Cuban Migratory System, so they can verify your identity in hours.

Cubans will get out any way they can. Once they are out, they just keep doing what they have done since they have been born: FIGHT TO SURVIVE. Canada is a great idea, but it would cost money. You have to create an account in Canadian dollars in a Canadian bank. You need to pay money for the English test, plus the fees to the Canadian Embassy. Then there is a medical exam and the "freedom card"—the exit visa—from the Cuban government, plus some fees to legalize extra documents, like your university degree, birth certificates and marriage or divorce certificates.

The news that you're coming back is fantastic. So, as soon as you have the program, tell me so I can organize my time at the office. Remember, this tour-guide job is crazy, and it's hard to make plans. I probably will take a couple of days off, but you also may have activities, and both of us need to be free. Okay? I won't say goodbye. Keep smiling.

November 27, 2004: I don't see any way of getting a tourist visa for the U.S. You can sometimes get a special visa to visit family in the U.S., but they must be parents, brother or sister, or close relatives. Cubans must have a sponsor, someone who will pay for the trip and take responsibility for the Cuban.

There are also visas for political refugees, Cuban who are being persecuted by the Cuban authorities because of their political activities against the government. In that case, you have to prove that you are really a "dissident."

I thought that I could organize a trip abroad and stay in a third country, find a job, and legalize my documents. Then I would be allowed to travel to Cuba with my Cuban passport and visit my family. I first thought about Europe, but I lost the connections I had. The European embassies ask too many questions about the sponsor, especially about tax payments and employment, and people don't like to give such details.

You know that Natasha and I are legally divorced. This was part of a plan we had for me to make a *mariage blanc*, a fake marriage, but it didn't work.

Actually, for the Canadian thing, Natasha and I have been discussing the advantage of getting re-married. It makes more sense for the future.

I can't wait to see you and talk more about all this. It may be difficult for you to think like a Cuban father forty years old, but when a door opens to the future, which is also the future of the family, we don't think about when it'll be possible to come back. We hope it will happen and we believe it will happen. It is simple: There is no future here.

I love you. P.S. The phone lines are really funny. Don't panic. We're here, like we say in Cuban Spanish, *vivito y coleando*, alive and moving. Kiss.

December 1, 2004: Things here are getting rougher by the day. The government has no money to carry on its "social projects." Of course they are always blaming the embargo. In terms of domestic politics there are signs of desperation, like removing an accounting director with twenty years of experience to put a party official who knows shit about economics in charge. This is the beginning of the end, but the regime is still pretending that we have a smooth economy. They have liberated five prisoners of that famous group of the seventy-five journalists who went to jail for their activities against the government. The virtual economy we have here can literally collapse in a blink. That will bring chaos and militarization at the same time. The Old Man probably will have a heart attack when he realizes he just lost the game. There is a fake *moral revolucionaria*, but when you talk to people on the street, you realize that everyone is just trying to figure out the next move. My mother is an economist, and she came home today from her part-time job sounding concerned about what she saw there. She also has friends in the Ministry of Culture, and the news about the lack of money is everywhere and is frightening.

I actually have an idea that would probably make my trip much easier and faster. I have been studying Canada, and definitely it seems to be the best choice. It is possible to do it being present in Canada myself. People living in Canada can apply for a permanent work visa. Once you have a job offer, money in the bank and your body there, it has to be much easier to pass all the formalities. If I get a tourist visa and have contacts in Canada who would "officially" take care of me for a while, I can renew my visa for a longer time and apply for permanent residency sur place. You can come to Canada to visit, and we both can figure out any future plans.

To get a tourist visa, I need a Canadian citizen to write a formal "invitation letter." As a tour guide, speaking English and French, and having a family (good reasons to come back), I don't see how they can deny me the visa.

If any of your friends or relatives in Canada will officially sponsor my trip as a tourist that would be

great. We have a saying here, "The worst negotia-
tion is the one you don't do."

I contacted a friend who lived in Montreal, a Jewish immigrant
from an Arab country, and she agreed to help by sponsoring Teseo.

December 2, 2004: Well, I see your friend in Canada
is ready to start. This is something that makes me
feel confident and sure. Natasha and I have discussed this choice a lot, and we agree that the faster
the better. We know how things can get torn apart
down here, and the future looks darker and darker.
Our Internet connection is having "natural" diffi-
culties, so don't get anxious if some days go by
without hearing from us. I have the documents I
need for the temporary visa application. I have been
talking with friends trying to understand what to do
once I am in Canada. We will discuss that in two
weeks. I am trying to set up a plan, and I pray for
these two months to pass quickly. Once your friend
is ready to go to the Cuban Consulate for the papers, I will start the countdown for my trip out of
the "cave." Being honest with you, I have a mix of
feelings right now. Some are very pleasant, and
some are uncertain. I think that the real possibility
of going out opens a hole in the dark wall that surrounds me, and it gives me happiness and courage,
but it's still just a possibility, and I will need patience
to hold on and keep waiting for the real fact that
your friend does what we need her to do. It's a hard
thing to know how dependent I am (and you as well)
on someone else's decisions and actions. Don't get
me wrong, but we need your friend to be there. I
was looking at your schedule for the trip, and except
for two days you'll be pretty busy. I am thinking
about asking my boss for a week off, alleging per-

sonal problems, so I can be at home all the time just waiting for your call to appear wherever you are in Havana so we can spend some time together. Kisses.

December 30, 2004: I have made contact with a friend in the Canadian Embassy. He's going to help with the paper work once I am ready to apply for the visa. He just needs to know when your friend is going to visit the Cuban Consulate. Isn't it great? I believe we must get started right after the New Year celebrations. What do you think?

The weather here is awful. Rainy, chilly, and impossible to drive along the Malecón. The waves are really big. Kiss you. Kiss you. Love.

IX

The Countdown Continues

My friend in Montreal came through and carried out her part of the plan. The invitation letter was on its way to Cuba.

January 4, 2005: Well, I feel rare. Having accomplished the first and most important step of this trip is like starting to climb a mountain that represents a big challenge. But I feel so sure about this, and also secure because having you at the other side is probably the biggest support. I don't know, there are so many feelings all together, and I feel optimistic.

Then, where have you been? I know it's all my fault. The end of this year was so busy for me. I was with a small group—eight people—but it was complicated because it meant full-time every day, counting two days out of town. These people were very nice, but the youngest was seventy-two and the oldest eighty-five. My biggest concern was to keep them away from all the obstacles that exist in Cuba's streets. They all wore hearing aids, so my efforts to make them understand were really big. Sometimes I had funny moments, having all my comments twisted just because they misheard a key word in my speech.

Let me give you an example. We were talking a little bit about the latest issue between Cuba and the U.S. government, which is the story of the number "75" at the American Embassy building. We went there because they wanted to take pictures. I am not sure if you are au courant so I will explain. The American Embassy, as usual, put Christmas-related stuff up, but this year they added a big sign with the number "75," in honor of the seventy-five prisoner-dissidents. Then the Cuban side of the plaza outside the U.S. Special Interests Section put huge signs with posters of the Iraq tortures by the American soldiers and a big swastika, facing the main entrance of the building. After thirty minutes visiting the area and taking pictures, we went back to the bus. Then, one of the old men asked me, "Okay, so why did the Cubans put the sign with the number '75' on the American side?" I was astonished. I couldn't believe my ears. I repeated that the "75" was put up there by the Americans to make trouble with the Cuban government. He stared at me a second and said, "Okay! Now I understand everything you said."

My goodness.

So you will understand how exhausted I was when I came home every single day. What I want most is to get online with you and chat. We must keep trying. This week I am off so I think we may have a chance to talk. Big kiss to you from your brother, Teseo.

February 3, 2005: This week I will make contact with the Cuban Foreign Affairs Ministry. I'm trying not to be desperate. Natasha just arrived from the doctors—routine consultation. Everything is fine, but the baby is pushing down, so she must stay quiet. That puts me in the position of big responsibility because we're not going to share the housework for this month. I will be very busy every day. Besides, next week is a free week at school. We're going to have my little boy around the whole day at home, and that means I must be a super papa and a super husband.

February 5, 2005: It seems there is a misunderstanding. I haven't received the letter yet. What I know is that the letter is in Cuba, somewhere between the Cuban Foreign Affairs Ministry and the international law firm that must assess it as a valid, true, legal document. I know for you guys all this sounds like Mars or Neptune, but in Cuba, everything is like outer space. I live on another planet.

The invitation letter is an official document issued by a Cuban consulate abroad, and because they're a branch of the Cuban Foreign Affairs Ministry, they send the documents through the pouch to some office in Havana that belongs to that ministry. Once in Cuba, the Foreign Affairs Ministry must send via mail that official invitation letter to the Cuban international law firm called Consultoria Juridica Internacional, which is the office authorized to validate the invitation letter issued by the Cuban consulate abroad.

After that long voyage, the interested person (the Cuban citizen invited) is officially notified via mail about the validated invitation letter and then must be present to collect it and start the rest of the process to apply for a visa to the inviting country.

So right now, the letter is somewhere between the Foreign Affairs Ministry and the law firm. I am tracing it just to intercept the letter and try to make the process shorter. It's good to know that the letter is here in Cuba, because at a given moment it will come into my hands.

February 19, 2005: Good news—I got the invitation letter. Next week I will start the process with my tour company, which is to request permission to travel. They must send a document that will be part of my application. I think the whole process, including the Cuban immigration permit, might take two more months, so probably I must be ready to travel in June. We have an appointment with a notary to get re-married next Thursday, and I have to revalidate my passport to be useful for two more years.

March 7, 2005: Now that I am in the middle of the process, I can't stop thinking how it will be. The very good reasons I have to keep going with my plans are also reasons not to. I hope you understand this. Having a family is a big thing, and my most encouraging thought is that I am doing this for them.

The Cuban reality is going down hill faster and faster, and I don't feel very optimistic about the coming disaster. Sometimes I feel sad, not for me personally. On the contrary, I feel very lucky to have found someone to help us come out of the mud. I don't want you to be worried. I'm okay and ready to go ahead.

March 18, 2005: We have a daughter! I don't have to tell you how I feel. The very same day she was born, I got the letter from my tour company. So I am ready to start the third step, which is to apply for a visa at the Canadian Embassy. I start this week and will keep you updated. So drink some rum to celebrate.

April 4, 2005: Cuba is going through a "new" wave. Fidel is developing a weekly program on TV. He is applying new methods to call for calm and confidence. Finally, the Government is accepting certain realities. Fidel is reading some opinions, like this: "Fidel is crazy. He is making too many promises." Another says, "Fidel needs to sweep the corruption away." Then, after reading each opinion, he makes endless comments explaining this and that, the causes of this mistake or the mistake made by some leader. The impression is that he's following Hugo Chávez' method of addressing the people. I don't have to tell you that there is both skepticism and optimism. I might trust him if I weren't so convinced that Cuba's reality will not change.

There is a funny joke going around about Fidel's weekly program. A guy is watching Fidel on television, and he says to his wife, "Hurry up, hon, Fidel is going to show us how to make a batido of mamey without milk, without fruit, and without a blender."

There have been some changes in the monetary policy. The Cuban peso was revalued last week. Now the rate is twenty-four to one convertible, and for 100 U.S. dollars you will have eighty-six convertibles. The new policy is to get rid of the U.S. dollar economy and get closer to the European market. The Chinese government is also getting very close to Cuba. This is just a re-edition of the strong economic dependency, which is a curse for us. It seems we're going back to the times when we depended on the U.S.S.R. Now the savior is China. Things won't change. There is no future at all.

April 12, 2005: You asked about health care and Natasha's experience in the hospital. Okay, these are mostly empirical observations because it's impossible to find real statistical data, only the official figures. In general, the health system in Cuba is very advanced compared to many other systems around the world. The big issue here is not the system itself but the way the bureaucracy handles it, and the eternal problem of salaries, which creates big contradictions within the personnel, doctors, nurses, and all the rest. Behind that we have the problem of medicine stocks, the lack of materials in the labs, and the lack of raw materials to produce medicine.

The Cuban system is based on ethical values, but here physicians do not get paid as they do in many other countries. As a state responsibility, medical care has to be free, and it has been free in Cuba since 1959. No payments are required at all. From emergency rooms to the most complicated surgery, everything is absolutely free. The government pays for everything, and you don't need to pay insurance to cover medical expenses. Professionals are paid a salary, and they are supposed to have a very high social position.

In the '80s, the government established an exception for plastic surgery when it's not a medical need or because of an accident. Also, we pay for all medicine, except what is provided during hospital stays. We don't pay for hospital beds and food, or for nursing care in a hospital. In principle, this system is very fair, except for doctors and nurses, because their salaries don't pay the general expenses a regular Cuban has. This is a problem for every single Cuban professional working for the government. Paying for medicine is a funny contradiction because whatever you pay is out of your own pocket, and there is no refund system.

During the '90s, in the Special Period, everything started to change. All the facilities deteriorated. Professionals left for any other job where they could earn dollars. Now the health system workers have the same problems as most Cubans. They don't make enough from their salaries, so corruption is a part of life. They sell medicine from the hospital's stocks. They sell the material from the laboratories. They sell their shifts to make more money.

It is forbidden by law for doctors to find a job in tourism. So they buy false papers for some other profession, or they declare that they are merely medical technicians. It's all very demoralizing and frustrating. The rest of the personnel—cleaning, maintenance, repair, etc.—also ran away to find jobs in the tourist sector.

In the second half of the '90s, the government created Servimed, an institution from the Health Ministry, to provide medical services to tourists in hotels and dollar clinics. It started a race to have a job in those places because they could make tips in hard currencies. I don't have to tell you that the working conditions in these clinics are awesome.

Also, the medical personnel (lab technicians, X-ray technicians, etc.) play a big role in the corruption. If you need an X-ray, they will find a way to make you pay something. There are long lines, or apparent technical problems with the equipment that are "magically" solved with five convertible pesos.

The quality of the medical system is now very bad. There is deception, corruption, desertion, demoralization, lack of supplies, bad working conditions, and health facilities in very bad shape. Now the government is trying to create new facilities and restore the existing ones, but I think their efforts will not make any progress.

In Cuba, not having to pay insurance is a big relief. But it works like blackmail from the government, because we have to be "good sheep." Anyway, the quality of medical care is not that good. Because with "equality," everybody has the same access, and because it's free, people go to see a doctor for anything. There are long lines, and fifty percent of the patients do not actually need to see a doctor. In Cuba, if you have a headache, you go see a doctor. Why not, it's free.

In America, things are going wrong with the health system, I guess. The privatization of medical insurance is a problem. I wouldn't mind paying insurance, but the problem is to whom. Whatever we pay is used by the government in unknown ways, a problem of no public control of budgets. We can't discuss where the money goes. In America, as a taxpayer, you can complain if you think they're spending your money the wrong way. I know you need press support and a lobby, but here, there's no chance at all.

I also think it's a matter of political culture. Here, people are not used to managing their own lives, one of the big problems of a planned society. Everything is done for you, all set up, and people just have to behave. But the final result is a strong individualism. After generations of failure, people lose faith in the system and survive at any cost, including others' pain. It's impossible for Cuba to have an independent, strong economy. Just look at our history. First we were dependent on the U.S., then the U.S.S.R., now China and Venezuela.

That was the same problem in England, 500 years ago, and that's why they developed such an open system, where economists and specialists could give the queen their opinions, and she would listen. We have a king, but he doesn't listen to anybody. That's the big difference. If he's right, good; if he's wrong, we're all fucked up.

Anger? Maybe. You know what I think. Life is too short, and personal responsibilities with the family are more important than becoming a hero.

P.S. When Natasha was at the hospital, we had to bring everything, our own sheets and towels, our own food, and cigarettes and coffee for the nurse, just in case.

April 15, 2008: Okay, I don't know what to say right now. I was denied the visa. Honestly, I was never sure about being accepted. This is all part of being Cuban. We are less than third-world citizens. We are the end of the world. I feel really bad and so sorry for you and your friend. Please talk to her because I don't want to do it right now. The reasons: "Your ties to your country of residence/citizenship balanced against factors which might motivate you to stay in Canada." This is from a sheet of paper they gave me after three hours of waiting. They also added my "current employment situation and remuneration" and my "personal assets and financial status." These points were just added to cover the decision. There were three old people who were affirmative and another young guy, like me, who was also denied. What a coincidence!

So, Sis, I need a break right now. I am a little bit confused. I'm tired, angry. What can I say? I feel humiliated. This is a fucking prison. But we can't give up. We will have to come up with a different plan. I have investigated all the possibilities in many different countries. Canada is the best choice. There are other ways, like applying for permanent residence, but it costs more money.

Or I could stay here and get another job, maybe go back to the Foreign Ministry. They need personnel. I would have to close my eyes and ears, but it would be easier now that I'm older. But there is a big contradiction. If I change to another job, I will not make as much money. And now I have two children, and a mother who is retired and on a pension. And there isn't that much money coming in from tourism either.

Also, we need a bigger house. If I have to stay, I must think about that seriously. Then if things get better for traveling, you could come here more often and stay with us.

April 19, 2005: We have a saying in Cuba: "Dios aprieta, pero no ahoga. God squeezes, but doesn't choke." It happens that someone who works at the Canadian Embassy was a classmate of Natasha's. Last night Natasha called her, and they talked for almost two hours. Among the things she said was that in the four years she's been working at the embassy, she hasn't seen too many young people getting a temporary visa. The official policy is to deny temporary visas to Cubans. They want Cubans to apply for full immigration. They are seeking well-educated people for the "skilled worker immigration program." She said not to feel bad at all. She strongly recommended that we apply for permanent residence. This is the "long" process. Natasha's friend said that if we decide to start, she would help us with all the paperwork.

I've been thinking a lot. Natasha and I have discussed a strategy, and we want to start the long process for the whole family. It makes a lot of sense in terms of being together as a family from the very beginning. Most important, we are thinking about our children's future. It depends on what you think.

May 1, 2005: You are perfectly right. We must try all the chances. Natasha and I have been talking a lot about all this and the changes it would bring to our lives. Personally, I have always been ready to go, not her. Now she realizes that the future of our children is very insecure, and she understands that even in the spiritual part of life, there are things that we won't have, never ever, in this country under this regime, and our kids will be as poor as we are. This is what I call "lack of a future."

Next week we start with the photos and the certificates. We think we can have all the papers ready by the end of June or early July for the Canadian Embassy. Then they take four weeks to give you an answer. We could have that answer by August, but it will also be summer break, and the Embassy might reduce their staff then. We also have to get passports for the children. So, when you come in August, there will be a chance to have a "yes" or "no" from the Canadians. Once we have the visas we still have to apply for the "Freedom Card," the exit permit, to leave Cuba. There is always the possibility of being denied.

I also have to have the "Liberation Letter" from my boss. This is a document written and signed by the big chief where you work that says they don't have any reason to question your migration, that you didn't have access to sensitive information. I haven't talked to my boss yet. A good 100 Cuban convertible pesos as a "gift" will help me a lot, so I won't hesitate to give him a big "thank you" envelope. I have done it before. So in the future I can ask for my "liberation" once the Canadians accept me as an immigrant.

June 2, 2005: Our application for the Canadian Embassy is ready. We just finished it tonight. Everything seems to be okay. Tomorrow I will go to the bank to pay the fees. And then, next Monday, we will bring the papers to the Embassy. We might have an answer before you arrive, and I think we will have a great pretext to have a sip of rum together. Big kiss.

June 24, 2005: Vamos bien—We're doing fine—is the biggest joke in Cuba these days. The blackouts are doing perfectly well, I would add. You know, the worst is that you lose a sense of regular time. Yesterday, for instance, the power went off at 8:00 p.m., and we were without light until 11:30 (almost midnight). The heat and the mosquitoes are big enemies, and because nothing works, there isn't much to do. I'm using my Angolan technique of reading with a flashlight, and I'm sure the consequence for my eyes won't be very good.

Yesterday afternoon, it was announced that at 5:30 p.m. Fidel was going to make a special appearance on television. Everybody was expecting him to talk about the power generation problems and plans for importing electrical devices. I felt confident about it, so at 5:30 sharp, I sat down with my little radio and started to listen. He talked for two and a half hours about the medical and educational achievements of the Revolution. He read some opinions, complaints, and some optimistic comments, laughing at most of them, like he was saying, "You poor people, don't you know how difficult it is to manage a country?" But at the end, not a single word about the power problems. What are we supposed to think?

I'm not telling you this to make a crying report. You know me pretty well. This is just another drop in the glass of disillusionment.

I went to my office and talked to my boss. Things are a mess there; the disorganization is really big. I negotiated some free time, keeping the job. He doesn't want me to leave, but he understands that I don't feel very attracted to doing airport transfers all the time. I have some freelance work next month. Once we meet here, I will explain why I must keep my official connection with the tour company until the end. So, I am fine, we are fine, everything else is not fine.

On July 9, 2005, the first Atlantic hurricane of the season, Hurricane Dennis, hit the southeast of Cuba, killing ten people, damaging buildings, and knocking out power. Six hundred thousand people fled their homes.

July 10, 2005: Hi, there! We'll survive. We have power now, but it's been very unstable. Our best hope is to have enough to get some cold water and to keep the freezer with ice so we won't lose food. Today we had running water during the day, but we lack cooking gas.

There is a lot of devastation along the south of Cuba, from Cabo Cruz to Cienfuegos. Remember the Jagua Hotel? Swept away. Also the Trinidad del Mar. There is also a lot of destruction across Matanzas Province and east Havana. Dennis was like a big air strike. The national generation power system is cut in two. The distribution of power is unstable, but at least the phone system is still working.

At home we are safe, and all my family is fine.

July 12, 2005: We have news. Are you ready? We went today to the embassy. We passed the first step! The point is that we qualify. It means we have all the points in the required topics. Now they have to prepare our new documents. Then we send them to someone in Canada.

The process might take twelve months, which means next summer we would probably travel to Canada. Our friend in the embassy told us that they have a yearly quota for immigrants, and we are queued for the 2006 group. There is nothing to do but wait. I feel confident.

As you know me well by now, you can imagine how many ideas I have about this trip. So, for the short period of time you're going to be in Havana, we must talk a lot. Here things happen fast. The Big Boss could die just like that, or he might have a nightmare about the Canadian links with the U.S. government, so you never know. My point is that when the papers are ready, we are going, no matter whether it's winter, summer, or spring.

July 18, 2005: Well, after some days of madness, it seems that the national power generation system is getting more stable. We have had electricity for forty-eight hours now, but we still have the feeling of a blackout coming at any time. It's blackout paranoia. Anyway, things are fine except that I lost the freelance trip I had. They cancelled because of all the troubles they would face on their trip across the island. I would have earned as much as two months of work, so I don't feel very happy. Nevertheless, we still have some reserve.

Natasha will be able to go back to work in three months. At my office things are not good at all. Any other job wouldn't pay enough to keep buying our kids milk, so I have to stay as a tour guide where I have the possibility of making something extra in tips or commissions.

I'm making a detailed home accounting. I don't see a way to reduce our expenses without going into malnutrition. Another big expense is the car. This tiny old *cacharro* eats a lot of gas and oil. The best price on the black market is sixty or seventy cents a liter. When I can't find a black supply I must pay eighty-five cents in a government gas station. I have thought about selling the car. It could give us around 7,000 convertible pesos, and we would be covered for ten months. But we would also be spending a lot on transportation. Taking cabs would cost about as much or maybe more than what we spend on the car. Plus at certain times it's really hard to catch a cab. When we sold our first car, some time ago, I remember we had to take our boy to the hospital, and we went to catch a Cuban cab. The driver wanted us to pay for all the seats because the hospital wasn't on his line. Remember that the Cuban peso taxis have set routes across the city. If you go off the route you must offer an attractive price so the driver will take you. This must cover the potential amount he would make if he had kept his regular course. So then you have the nuisance of discussing the fare with the drivers and getting stuck somewhere because it's hard to catch a cab at certain times. So, selling the car is not a good idea yet.

Politically, things are not very happy. The Cuban government is making too many plans based on Venezuela, and that scares me to the bone. What's going to happen if Chávez dies, or gets killed, or simply loses the next election? We have been through that twice before: in the '60s, when the U.S. cut off ties with Cuba, and then in the '90s, after the Russian slaughter. Another Special Period can be possible only with a strong repression. There have been plenty of complaints against the government with all the power problems. You know my theory—that there will be a civil war when Fidel dies. So I'm praying for long life for Chávez and Fidel. Honestly.

I am filling my time with study, readings, and writings. I want to contribute my ideas about what would make a good society, for my children and for humans in general. To have lived in Cuba can be a unique opportunity to understand what is wrong with communism, but also what could be right with socialism, in terms of social justice, and so on. So I am using my waiting period to get more prepared to understand any further changes in my family life. You know, I feel committed to that, you included, of course. I have the feeling that it will be part of my payback to you. Real love, care for each other, and HOME, even within the natural distance between Canada and San Francisco. I see our lives tightened forever.

I have always had a strong interest in philosophy, sociology, and anthropology. That's why I see the filled part of the glass. My Cuban experiences are kind of unique for a society like Canada, and even more so for America. Reading has been the same as traveling for me. Also, talking, which has given me the chance to actually interview some of my clients, the people I have met as a tour guide. They have been like open pictures of their own realities, giving me a kind of outlook of how my life would be in such societies. So I welcome the culture shock. My best hope is that one day I will be able to write down all my thoughts and make a contribution, to help people avoid the same mistakes I have made.

July 21, 2005: They are trying to make us think there are no more problems. In Trinidad they have been out of power for two weeks. I know those areas like the palm of my hand, and I tell you, they live under a permanent hurricane. Trinidad is a crumbling city, despite what they show to tourists. I mean, the biggest hurricane of all has one name: Fidel.

X

Las Quimbambas

In August 2005 I got back to Cuba by volunteering with Earthwatch, a nonprofit organization that sends volunteers into the field to help scientists. I would be working with Cuban biologists who were studying the American crocodile in Las Tunas Province, in southeastern Cuba. I wasn't sure I would like this trip, since I was deathly afraid of crocodiles, but I figured it would give me more knowledge about the natural world in Cuba, and a chance to go off the usual tourist route. Teseo wanted to come with me, but it was impossible to arrange; we didn't even try. Teseo had a responsibility to his family and couldn't be gone for ten days, and he would need special permission from the Cuban government to go into the research area. Earthwatch volunteers had very specific visas that allowed us to work with the biologists.

I had one day in Havana before we left for the research station, and I planned to spend it with Teseo, going on a reconnaissance mission. We drove nine miles west of Havana to check out the Hemingway Marina as a possible escape route, in case Plan A, Canada, fell through. Plan B was my daredevil cousin, who had a boat moored in the Caribbean, and who volunteered to help smuggle Teseo off the island.

"There is an amusement park for Cubans right in the marina," Teseo told me. "Cubans get in all the time." But can they get out? I held my breath as we drove past the guard post at the entrance.

There was no problem driving in. Before going there I pictured the marina as a cute little port, but it was larger and more developed than I had imagined. It was also deserted. "That's because it's a Monday. The recreation area for Cubans is open only on weekends." There were four inlets where boats were moored, a lot of nice housing, even a hotel and restaurants.

Apparently you could sail right in. There were a few guards scattered around; they looked about fourteen years old. We chatted them up and had one of them take our photo standing in front of a car, before having lunch in a Chinese restaurant, where we were the only patrons. The marina was not exactly crawling with people or any activity that might provide cover; even so, I imagined a future visit when it would be possible to slip Teseo onto a yacht with the proper "tip" to the guards or even a bottle of rum to distract them.

It was hot and my face was turning bright red, so Teseo, concerned, stopped to pick up a bottle of cold water. We arrived back at his house, and the whole *familia* was waiting to greet us, including Teseo's mother, his sister, nephew, children, and the cat. I was particularly concerned about what Mom thought of me—this foreigner, taking her son away—but she greeted me warmly, thanked me for my empathy, and said she felt an affinity with me. She didn't speak English fluently, and my Spanish was marginal, but we immediately understood one another. At one point she literally gave me the shirt off her back, gifting me a woven shawl. I received other gifts from Teseo and Natasha—an old stamp album, a couple of woodcarvings. It amazed me that people with so little in the way of material goods were so rich in generosity.

As the family dispersed, Teseo, Natasha, and I had a chance to talk more seriously about Canada. They had filled out papers to open a bank account there, a necessary part of the process, and they entrusted these papers to me to take back and mail from the U.S., which would be quicker than mail from Cuba. Teseo, always organized, presented a spreadsheet detailing expenses, so we could further figure out financial logistics. Our plan was moving forward.

Leaving Havana after dinner, our Earthwatch group traveled by tourist bus to Jobabo, stopping along the highway to fill the gas tank, grab a sandwich and down a quick *cafécito*. These "dollar" stores gave us a chance to stock up on any essentials we might need for the days ahead: bags of powdered milk, snacks, and (for some) rum and beer.

We arrived at the town of Jobabo the next morning, at dawn, having spent the sleeping hours on the bus. We had a light breakfast at the home of one of the project scientists and then took a smaller van to the community of Manuel Zabalo, a village of about 800 inhabitants, situated near the northern reserve boundary. Here there was a crocodile farm, administered by the National Enterprise for the Conservation of Flora and Fauna, closely linked to the Monte Cabanaguan Wildlife Refuge, where we would be staying. We clambered onto another vehicle, an open-bed truck, pulled by a tractor, and bumped along a pot-holed, dirt road that took us to a strikingly different habitat—a large swath of tidal mud, with a watery swamp on the far side.

Now came the really hard part: crossing a makeshift bridge on foot, while carrying our luggage and supplies. It was somewhat terrifying and required very good balance, not my strong point. The bridge was narrow and was constructed of thin, uneven tree trunks laid crossways on a narrow support structure. It wasn't a long drop into the mud, but if you fell, not only would it be embarrassing, but also you'd also probably sink up to your waist in tidal muck. In addition, it was now high noon, and the heat and humidity increased the stress factor.

Some Cubans arrived from the far side to help us carry our gear and supplies. Obviously practiced at crossing the bridge, they picked up our suitcases and packages, balanced them strategically, and raced deftly across. The bridge was a quarter of a mile, and I breathed a big sigh of relief when I reached the end without mishap and stepped onto land. But we weren't done yet. The last leg of the trip was in small motorboats, and as we slipped into the mangroves, under a welcome canopy of shade, I had the first glimpse of the beautiful, bird-filled habitat in which I would be living for ten days.

It was peaceful on the water. Herons and other wading birds watched our progress. The head biologist used the time to tell us a little about the reserve.

We learned that the Monte Cabaniguan Wildlife Refuge comprised 14,000 hectares of the largest and most important wetland ecosystem of eastern Cuba. The major habitats in the area were mangrove swamp, estuaries, palm savannas, and tropical hardwood forest. It was an outstanding breeding ground for endemic and endangered wildlife, including Cuban iguanas, parrots, parakeets, Fernandina's flickers, whistling ducks, manatees, quail doves, flamingoes, and American crocodiles. The region sustained the largest local population of the American crocodile in the species' entire range.

Biologists had been doing research on the crocodiles since 1990. The general objective of the project was to obtain first-hand information on the status, life history, and ecology of the species for the design of a long-term management program for their conservation. Crocodiles played an important role in the ecology of the wetland habitat. They helped balance the complex life in the freshwater and estuarine systems. As predators at the top of the food chain, they ate a wide range of prey. As babies they were prey themselves, to feral pigs, turtles, fish, sea eagles and even other crocodiles. Crocodiles kept the wetland ecosystems healthy, and this meant the fisheries would also be healthy.

"Given that the American crocodile is the most widely distributed crocodile in the Americas, and an endangered one, this project has a high significance in the national and regional context," the biologist explained. "Earthwatch volunteers will assist us in a variety of practical research tasks during periods of very high working pressure, especially during the nesting and hatching seasons. Assignments will include participation in night spotlight counts, nest and hatchling surveys, capture, sampling, and tagging of juvenile and sub-adult crocodiles, and primary analysis of stomach contents."

While vividly imagining what "analysis of stomach contents" entailed, we emerged from the tangle of mangroves to arrive at a clearing; the sky was now visible, and we could see the mouth of the Cauto River with the sea beyond. There was our new home—the Miguel Alvarez del Toro Biological Station—sitting at the tip of a sandspit.

The research station consisted of a wooden building with a central community room, three bedrooms, a storeroom, and an outside porch with a dining table and chairs, facing the water. An open thatched-roof cooking shed was located a few steps away. The cook, prepared meals on a wood fire at one end of the room. There was space for a table and three chairs, a bar area, and a room with bunk beds for the camp staff. The common area had a television, which was shared by everyone in the community.

Behind the kitchen shack were two bathrooms, each with a toilet and shower, basically a pipe with cold water. Showers were most easily taken by the bucket method, to conserve water. We went outside, filled up a bucket through a spigot leading to a water container on top of the roof, and then went back inside to lather up and take our shower. We could also have the cook heat up the water on the wood fire, but this was a luxury I did without since it was hot and humid, and the cold water felt good.

The communal sink was outside between the bathrooms and the kitchen. Once a week huge containers of fresh water for cooking and bathing arrived by boat, and it was a major engineering feat to raise these containers and hook them up to the plumbing.

A solar cell panel provided electricity. There were lights in the bedrooms and fans to keep the mosquitoes at bay. The sand flies, however, were small enough to get through the holes of the mosquito nets. When it rained, huge hairy spiders appeared on the beds.

It was perfect. I was happy. To me, this environment was Paradise.

There were no cell phones, no traffic, and no pollution. Every morning, at 6:30 sharp, I awoke to the sound of a flock of pelicans diving for fish in the river. Their synchronized splashdown was my own personal symphony, my alarm clock. The sun was just coming up, and I could smell the strong coffee that was being brewed in the kitchen. I dressed quickly and went to stand near the fire in the kitchen, trying not to show my impatience as the cook strained the aromatic coffee through the cloth colander. The camp started to come alive with the sounds of others waking up, their talk and laughter. Sunrise over the river was spectacular.

I liked to sit at the kitchen table with the biologists, all of us savoring our *cafecitos*, huddled around the portable radio, listening to Radio Rebelde, which played wonderful music with occasional pauses for anti-imperialist rhetoric: "America is getting ready to invade Iran for the oil."

"We are tired of being on a war footing all the time," said one of the biologists. "We listen to this, and our blood pressure goes up. All we want is to have normal relations with the rest of the world."

One thing I liked about being at the station was the lack of tourist apartheid. The Cuban biologists slept in the same area as the Earthwatch volunteers. Some of us pitched tents out on the sand, which gave a bit of privacy, but when it rained at night, everyone scurried in to set up their tents in the dining room, or on the porch under the eaves. On certain mornings we were tripping over each other, but everyone was respectful, and the sense of camaraderie made it fun.

In the back room was a library of books brought in and left by various volunteers. There were the expected manuals describing the geology, plant, bird, and animal life in Cuba. But there was also a good collection of books that were banned, like George Orwell's *1984* and *Animal Farm*. Out here in the middle of nowhere—*las quimbambas,* as the Cubans said ("the place where the Devil doesn't even know his own children"), we were far away from the center of power, and far away from the prying eyes of the police. Or were we?

XI

Paranoia

There were many other Cubans in the camp whose reasons for being there were unclear to me, plus locals who appeared at different times. An incident occurred that made me wonder whether the camp was bugged, or at least the communal room in the station. Two windows separated this room from the porch, and the dining table and chairs were set up outside, since the evening breezes were so pleasant. Sometimes it was easier to climb through the windows to get back to our rooms than to go all the way around the table, having to push the chairs aside or disturb others, and then up the wobbly steps through the front door. So we all took to going in and out through the windows, which were pretty close to the floor.

One afternoon I climbed in from the outside and landed on someone's pack, which was directly under the window on the inside. I heard a muffled sound but chose to ignore it. After all, I didn't want to get caught snooping through someone else's possessions to see if I broke anything important. Later that day the director of the camp made a point of showing me his reading glasses, which were broken. Was it his pack I had stepped on? And if so, how did he know I was the one who broke his glasses? Was there a camera hidden somewhere in the room? Or was I just becoming paranoid?

My roommate was another matter. I knew she had recently resigned from the U.S. State Department, and I wondered what she was doing in Cuba, or, more accurately, why they let her in. She mentioned in passing that she had been stationed in Venezuela shortly before resigning, and she had been in Africa at the time the Cubans were fighting in Angola. Could it be that she was really C.I.A.? "Why did you resign from the State Department after that long career?" I probed.

"I really didn't agree with our government's policy any longer," she told me. I noted her copious consumption of alcohol, and the fact that she claimed not to know Spanish. "How could you be stationed in Venezuela without speaking Spanish?" An innocent enough question.

"I just was." But after she downed a few drinks of alcohol, I realized she understood everything the Cubans were saying, and she became pretty verbal in Spanish herself.

Given my radical past, it wasn't surprising that the F.B.I. had a file on me during the '60s and early '70s. In the '80s, I requested this file after the Freedom of Information Act was passed, and it was interesting to see what they knew and what they didn't know about me. Now, at dinner, we had a discussion about names and about being Jewish, and my roomie, who had been drinking for a while, suddenly became very coherent and focused on me. "What's your maiden name?" she asked, and without giving it a second thought, I told her. My F.B.I. file, of course, was under my maiden name.

Roomie confided to me that one of her close friends, a gay man whom she called her "husband," had been murdered, and his murderer was now about to be paroled. She wanted to write a letter to the judge detailing her reasons for opposing the parole, and I offered to help edit the letter. One afternoon she announced that she was not going into the field with us. "I need a break," she told the team leader. When we returned in the afternoon, she told me, "I had to borrow a page from your journal," and I said to myself, *Okay, so she read my journal.* She never asked for my help with the letter she prepared for the judge.

The team leader and I had a private conversation about her. "She used to work for the State Department," I began.

"I know," he said. "She had to fill out an additional form explaining why she wanted to come here, and she said she wanted to do a comparison between what was happening in Venezuela and

Cuba." He also noticed the discrepancies in her behavior. He also thought she was an American spy.

One afternoon, Roomie told me that another Earthwatch member was complaining that I spent too much time talking to the leader and that the others didn't have much of a chance to talk to him. This surprised me because, being younger and not really that interested in learning about Cuba, they spent a lot of their free time watching videos and talking to the younger people in the camp. So I decided to call Roomie's bluff and, before she could protest, I went to ask the other volunteer if she had, in fact, made this comment. She denied it, vehemently, and I believed her. "If you do feel that way, just come join us and participate in the conversation," I said. "I'm sure the leader would be delighted." Roomie didn't try to manipulate me again.

It was another night in the television room, and we were watching Castro congratulate the graduates of the Latin American Medical School. Elián Gonzáles, the young boy who was sent back to Cuba from Miami, was in the audience, obviously a privileged guest of Castro, his true "father." Hugo Chávez was there, all smiles, sharing the glory. Both he and Castro wore medals around their necks, presented by one of the students in a flowery speech. She approached the two men and symbolically entwined their individual medals around each other. They beamed at each other, charismatically. The crowd erupted on cue.

Roomie passed through the room with a drink in her hand, glanced at the television, saw Hugo Chávez, said, "My hero!" and continued on her way. For someone who was interested in Cuba-Venezuela relations, she didn't seem very interested in watching an event that would never be shown on American television. Personally, I found it fascinating.

Now Castro put on his reading glasses, fiddled with a few pieces of paper and began reading a lot of statistics about the school: the number of graduates, the cost—the man was enamored of numbers. He compared the cost of Cuban medical education to that in America, without, of course, mentioning the pay that doctors received in the U.S., or the fact that they were free to practice where they wanted.

His voice was weak; he fumbled with his reading glasses and seemed uncertain. Then Castro gave an aside: "But we are not here to discuss ideology." A collective groan went up from the Cubans in the television room; they knew what was coming. Castro removed his glasses, put his notes aside, and frowned at the camera. It was going to be a long night, and the regularly scheduled television programs would be pre-empted.

Castro launched into the same canned speech he always gave about the wonders of the Revolution and the Evil Empire to the North. His voice became stronger and more assured. He gesticulated wildly and glared into the camera. He went on like this for another hour, while the honored audience suppressed yawns. Somehow his manic ranting always reminded me of the old newsreels of Hitler.

It was time to eat dinner, and we rose from our chairs. One of the Cubans made a disdainful gesture toward the screen, as if to say "Bah, enough already!" But no one wanted to be the person who actually turned off the television! As we settled down at the dining table, Castro's voice boomed in the background, sucking all other speech into a black hole. We ate in silence.

We were all sitting around one afternoon, waiting for a thunderstorm to clear, and the leader told us a joke about an economist who was sent to Cuba by the C.I.A.: "The guy comes back and has to be hospitalized on a psychiatric ward. All he can say is, 'I don't get it! I don't get it!' The President of the U.S. goes to investigate. 'What don't you get?' he asks the economist. 'I don't get how things work in Cuba. It's not logical. The government says they have 100 percent employment, but no one works. They announce astounding production figures, but the shelves in the grocery stores are empty. People say they love the Revolution, but a lot of them are trying to leave the island. I don't get it! I don't get it!' "

"Here's another one," he continued. "Do you know about the three main achievements of the Revolution? Healthcare, education, and sports. Do you know about the three failures of the Revolution? Breakfast, lunch, and dinner." The leader and I had some good discussions about Cuba, when no one else was around. We usually sat outside on the steps and spoke in a low voice. He was afraid there might be listening devices in the main room. "The main problem with our system is motivation," he explained. "When you get paid the same amount whether or not you work hard, there's no incentive. I love my job and my family and could never leave Cuba, but I worry for my kids. Fortunately, they have no ambition.

"Also, I think it's stupid that we're not supposed to be associating with you," he went on. "They're afraid you might contaminate us with your ideas. Why couldn't it work the other way around? Couldn't we convince you that socialism works better than capitalism?" He spread his arms in a gesture of exasperation. But he didn't get a chance to elaborate on this subject. Someone was approaching; we had to stop talking.

For the first few days we studied the Cuban iguana, and part of our work was to find their nests, dig out eggs without breaking them, weigh and measure the eggs, and then return them to the nest. We traveled by motorboat into the mangroves and landed in a sandy area. Probing the ground for eggs, we tried not to break them, and we hoped we wouldn't encounter an irate female iguana. They had very sharp claws and could inflict injury. We also captured a couple of adult iguanas to take back for measuring and weighing at the station. Trussed up and immobilized, they were passed around so we could take photos of each other posing as intrepid iguana hunters.

"Well," said our leader one morning. "I know you're frustrated because we haven't been doing much with the crocodiles. We're past the hatching season and it's not yet the egg-laying season; that's the reason. But today we're going to start preparing the ground for the egg-laying." The whole crew, all the staff and volunteers, traveled in two boats to a raised part of land. Nearby was a good supply of sand, and we filled our buckets with as much as we could carry to transport it to the chosen ground. The idea was to give the female crocodiles a good place to lay their eggs, a place that was far enough above the water line so their nests wouldn't be flooded by the incoming tide. Although it was hot and the eggs might bake, the female crocs kept watch on their eggs and even urinated on top of the sand to keep their nest moist. "They're good mothers," someone said.

We formed a bucket brigade, passing the buckets hand over hand, rotating tasks from time to time, and our work was done quickly. "That's the fastest we ever did this," said our leader, impressed.

One major problem in the mangroves was the lack of communication between the two boats. There was no way of knowing where the other boat was, and if we got separated, we had to wait for it. This could be solved with walkie-talkies, and I resolved to bring a couple to the scientists at some point in the future. (I discovered later that it was illegal to bring communication equipment into Cuba, and Cuban Customs confiscated the walkie-talkies on my next trip. I filled out a form explaining what they were for and was promised that one of the biologists could pick them up, but when he arrived to claim them, they couldn't be found. They had been lost forever in the regime's kleptocracy.)

Meanwhile, the birding was spectacular. Roseate Spoonbills were nesting, and one of the biologists offered to take me closer to the nesting site. He traveled quickly and easily across the surface of the swamp. I took one step, sank into the muck, and had to be pulled out. "You have to walk fast," he explained, but I never did master the knack of walking on tidal mud. I had to view the nests from a distance, with my binoculars. As we motored back to the camp, flocks of Flamingoes took off in a flash of coral and pink.

We always wore life jackets on the boats. "Do you like your life jacket?" the leader asked me. He chuckled.

"Sure. Why?" I didn't quite get the joke.

"If you go into the water, it will hold you up." He smiled. What was I missing? "Check out the name on the label."

The label on the life jacket said *Castro*. Okay, got it.

The next day we captured a couple of juvenile crocodiles; that is, the staff captured them. We, the volunteers, were not allowed in the water. The crocodiles floated soundlessly, looking like logs, with only their eyes visible as two bumps above the water line. The biologists slipped into the water, which was up to their necks, and spread a net around the crocodiles. But the crocs disappeared; they managed to get under the net. "These crocodiles have been to the university!" one of the biologists remarked. "¡Son academicos!" But then the director of the reserve camouflaged his hat with mangrove leaves and swam slowly up to a crocodile and slipped a noose over its neck.

Once it was in the boat with its snout tied securely, this croc was no longer dangerous. We passed it around for photo opportunities, and, miraculously, a bottle of rum and a thermos of coffee appeared. We all celebrated the first crocodile catch of the week.

At night we went out by boat with a spotlight, to locate more crocodiles. We took turns sitting on the bow of the boat, shining the light over the water, sweeping it back and forth until we saw the tell-tale, red eye-shine. That way we located more crocodiles for the next day's catch. They would be measured, weighed, and inspected at the station, and later released. There was a method for recording the date of capture, which involved notching the hardened scales on the croc's back, so it could be identified if we came across it in the future.

Coming back from any boat trip involved laying out our shoes and socks to dry, and one day I noticed that my sneakers had disappeared. There was an immediate panic in the camp, and the whole staff dropped what they were doing to look for my shoes. "It's not really that serious," I offered, embarrassed. "I have another pair."

"Yes it is!" said our leader. "We can't have anyone stealing in the camp." My shoes were never found, and it made me suspicious of every person I saw in the camp. I checked to make sure my passport and important documents were still secure. I had stashed them in my suitcase, which was under my bed, so someone would have had to enter the room. I was especially concerned about those important papers from Teseo. Fortunately, nothing was missing.

We had accomplished a lot on our research project, and I had learned a lot more about Cuba. Now a hurricane was forming, and there was concern that we wouldn't be able to leave. Someone had a short-wave radio and kept us posted on the news coming from Miami.

It was pouring rain, and I worried about Teseo's official Canadian papers getting wet. I had them wrapped in plastic bags and stuffed into my suitcase, but with the rain and the rising tide, I feared that the cabin would be flooded. I told one of my Earthwatch friends about Teseo, and he promised that if anything happened to me on this trip, like being eaten by a crocodile, he would make sure the papers got to their destination.

The last night of the project the leader gathered us together for a goodbye party. We broke out what was left of the rum and beer and drank a toast to friendship between the Cuban and American people. We had a good laugh singing songs to each other.

Arriving in Havana late the next night, we exited the bus to a heavy downpour. The Canadian papers were now in my backpack, which got soaked on the short run from the bus to the front door of the hotel. I was relieved that the papers stayed dry.

The next morning I was up early, packed and having my morning coffee in the hotel, when I was informed that one of the younger volunteers had been robbed in Old Havana the night before. We all shared what we had left of our money so he could pay the airport tax and get out of the country. The trip ended on this sour note.

Roomie was going on to another volunteer job at Volcanoes National Park in Hawaii. When I later told this to a friend whose sister worked in the State Department, he said, "This is where all C.I.A. agents go to be debriefed." But he was someone who never let the truth get in the way of a good story, so I wasn't sure I could believe him.

XII

Campeones de la Dignidad

As the year 2006 began, Teseo and I continued to stay in touch by email, and we both went through a range of emotions in anticipation of the family's arrival in Canada. Teseo was certain that they would be able to emigrate. I couldn't quite relax, fearing that the Cuban government wouldn't grant the required exit permits, even if Canada had given approval. Teseo made light of my worry.

"We Cubans have that fear embedded. I have heard stories of people being called back from the plane to the airport, right before take-off. That's part of the government's game. There's a joke about a guy who enters the airport by jumping over a fence, illegally. He tries to get to an old aircraft, and a guard tells him, 'Hey! What are you doing? You can't fly that airplane; it could fall down any time anywhere!' The guy says, 'Right. That's all I need. Anywhere but here.'"

We both knew there would be a price the family would pay for emigrating. "I have to make a big effort to get used to the idea of leaving loved personal stuff behind. And I won't be able to sell my car to have extra money for the trip. Properties like homes and cars must be given back to the government if they've been owned in the past five years, from the moment one presents the official documents to emigrate. At least the house is in my mother's name. But I feel sick about the car. We counted on that money to cover the expenses for the final arrangements and to leave some for our families. Mom told me to see this as just another fee for freedom. It's part of the price, but it sill hurts."

At the same time, Teseo felt "very lucky, because now all my plans include my family with me, and I can believe there will be a different future for our children." The fact that they could all emigrate together and give each other love and support during the adjustment made me more confident that they would succeed in a new land.

In March 2006, I went back to Cuba with Earthwatch to work on the crocodile project. It was now the dry season, cool enough that we needed blankets at night. The stars were spectacular; I could actually see the edge of the Milky Way. Besides me, there were only two other female volunteers this time, and there were fewer Cubans in the camp. It was much easier to organize boat trips, and there was no heavy drinking or interpersonal drama. We were a very compatible group.

Our leader was telling *piñero* jokes—what we might call "Polish" jokes—which made fun of people from the province of Pinar del Rio. "There was a taxi driver from Pinar del Rio who picked up a couple of passengers. When they got out of the cab, he noticed they had left a 100-dollar bill on the back seat. 'Oh,' he said. 'The next people who get into my cab are going to be very lucky!'"

He then informed us we would have a visitor who wanted to see what we were doing, someone who fought with Fidel in the Sierra Maestra and had access to materials the research station needed for a better pipeline to the water. I took this announcement as a warning. *Please don't talk politics with this guy, Regina.* He turned out to be a handsome, charming, and aristocratic man, who owned a quarter-horse ranch in the province. Joining us in the field, he absorbed a lesson in how to extract crocodile eggs carefully, without breaking them. He joked and flirted with us and invited us all to come ride his horses. He kissed one of the young women good-bye on the cheek; I felt jealous.

One of the volunteers kept singing the crocodile song from *Peter Pan*:

"Never smile at a crocodile.

No, you can't get friendly with a crocodile.

Don't be taken in by his welcome grin.

He's imagining how well you'd fit within his skin."

It was contagious, and soon we were all singing it.

The other volunteer heard me talking about the crocodiles' *radio bemba*—the females always seemed to know where to lay their eggs. Somehow they communicated. We had the radio on, and she asked, "Where can I find *radio bemba* on the dial?" We all had a good laugh, and someone explained to her that this was just an expression meaning gossip, word of mouth, not a real radio frequency.

"We're very tense right now, because of what's happening," a biologist confided. Was it something political? No. Cuba had just won the World Baseball Classic semifinals against the Dominican Republic, and there was a lot of anticipation and excitement in the camp. We stopped work early so we could gather in the television room to watch the game, along with the local fishermen. Spirits were high, but Cuba lost the final game against Japan for the championship.

The next night there was a ceremony on television, with Fidel and other officials welcoming back the exhausted-looking Cuban baseball team. This event took place in a packed stadium at the *Ciudad Deportiva* in Havana. The words *Campeones de la Dignidad* flashed continuously on the screen. This was how Fidel referred to the returning baseball players. Why were they Champions of Dignity? Because they didn't defect. As if they could have with all the coaches and doctors constantly surrounding them, Fidel's son, Tony, included. I later read that the players were pretty much sequestered in their hotel rooms, under strict curfew, guarded day and night. But yes, they did all return, and Fidel was hailing this as the real victory for the team and thus for the nation, which meant for him, personally.

Castro looked pretty spry. He gave the players individual attention as they mounted the stage. He shook their hands, talked to them, and punched some of them on the chest in a *machismo* display of affection—it was all very Latin and appealing. The players were presented with a bat inscribed *Felicidades*, and then they filed off the stage. The camera filmed the scene from every possible angle. Above the podium was a giant Cuban flag; an even bigger photo of Ché, the famous Korda photo, hung above the flag.

Castro rambled on, reading from notes at first, almost losing his voice, which sounded weaker and more hoarse than usual. He talked about what good patriots the baseball players were to come back. He talked, and then he talked some more.

As the night wore on, Fidel left his notes aside to fume about the usual subjects, and many of the baseball players were caught napping by the camera. The Cubans watching all this with me were visibly annoyed; they would rather be finding out what happened in the latest episode of *La Cara Oculta de La Luna*, The Dark Side of the Moon, a soap opera about a gay man with AIDS.

The research station had become a special place for me, and I would have continued going back to work there indefinitely. However, at the end of 2006, Earthwatch lost its official U.S. license to send volunteers to Cuba; nor would the Cuban government give civilian tourists permission to enter the reserve. The leader tried to wangle me permission to come in as a designated "crocodile specialist" to work with the biologists, but it wasn't possible. And so I saw my dream of returning to my beloved mangroves spiraling away from me, like a receding galaxy in an ever-expanding universe.

In November 2006, Teseo wrote me to say that things were moving ahead. "I spoke with our friend at the Canadian embassy, and she thinks that by mid-December they will start calling those who are ready to go forward in the emigration process. We have a very good chance of being in that group, because we are just waiting to hear from the embassy to begin the last steps: our medical exams, arrival fees, and the Cuban migration formalities. She said that they are anxious to start because they're backed up with the quotas they're allowed. That's the reason for the delay. So at the beginning of 2007, they'll have quotas available again, and they'll start with those who have already qualified. So we're very excited and are just waiting for November to go by fast and see if December brings us good news."

XIII

Picasso and the Ambassador

On my next trip to Cuba, I stayed at a hotel closer to where Teseo and Natasha lived. I didn't like Old Havana, the tourist part of town. It was beautiful but seemed artificial, and I was tired of being accosted by the street hustlers who lurked outside the hotels, waiting for prey.

At the house we celebrated with a cocktail of pineapple juice and vodka. The more I got to know this close-knit family, the guiltier I felt about breaking them apart. My guilt increased the closer we got to our goal.

Natasha only recently had told her parents she was planning to leave. "It was creating a lot of tension having to keep it secret," she told me. Her father, a *militante*, had a fierce reaction. "You will not survive outside Cuba," he warned. "People outside don't care about each other at all. If you fall down on the street no one will even stop to help you."

"My mother told me she was having chest pains," Natasha added, "threatening to have a heart attack. I finally had to put my foot down and demand a family meeting. I explained everything and reassured them that we would still be a close family. My father's main fear was that he wouldn't be able to see the children any more. He's a big family man."

"What's the latest with the Canadian Embassy?" I asked.

"They interviewed me for two and a half hours!" saidTeseo.

"They made me take an English test," added Natasha, "and this really annoyed me since I studied English at school." In fact, her English was better than Teseo's. "We also had to correct the name of Teseo's father on his birth certificate and pay more fees. Everything has to be perfect, and you have to have conclusive proof for everything." This phrase, "conclusive proof," was now part of their vocabulary. It became a private joke among us.

"I had to bring a whole truck-load of documents over to the embassy," said Teseo, conjuring up a comical image. I could see that this lengthy process was designed to eliminate people who weren't seriously committed to emigrating or didn't have the funds to jump through all the hoops. We just had to hang in and continue, no matter how long it took. I wasn't about to give up at this point, and neither were they.

Teseo and I drove to Jaimanitas, west of Havana, to meet Fuster, an artist who billed himself as "The Picasso of the Caribbean." As we approached his house I saw that the whole neighborhood around it was also a canvas for his work. A cement wall with a curvy top ran along the sidewalk. It was painted green and plastered with ceramic tiles, creating a colorful, fairy-tale décor of sculpture and art.

We entered the house itself through an arch and walked down a mosaic-cobbled path, past a large swimming pool and patio, all surrounded by a wall that was decorated with sculpture. The effect was a riot of color and creativity, quite a contrast to the drabness outside, a visual shock that delighted the eye.

Teseo went ahead to make sure Fuster was home, but suddenly came running back, looking concerned, blocking my way. "Regina, Regina, the American ambassador is here. PRETEND YOU'RE CANADIAN!"

"What? Why should I? I'm here legally. I don't have to pretend anything." As we entered the patio, there he was: Michael Parmly, tall, relaxed, the official representative of the U.S., with a woman (his wife?), and a younger woman (his daughter?) in tow.

He was in the process of saying goodbye to Fuster, who then introduced us. "You are Canadian," he stated.

"No, I'm American, from San Francisco."

"Hmm. Regina, from San Francisco." He cocked his head, mulling this over, and I imagined he was making a mental note to check me out when he got back to the office, as if it would be important to him. Teseo stood by, shifting his weight on his feet and drawing repeatedly on his cigarette.

"Are you an artist also?" I prompted, pretending I had no idea who he was.

"No, I'm just a bureaucrat," he replied, smiling, and he then exited the premises with his entourage.

Fuster and Teseo let out their breath simultaneously. "What a bastard," Fuster said. Teseo nodded in agreement. I, on the other hand, had a desire to spend more time talking to Michael Parmly.

"I should have invited him to lunch. I'd love to hear his take on what's going on here."

"No, no, no," Teseo warned. "Are you crazy? You don't want to argue with him about the embargo."

"What makes you think I'd argue with him? I think it would be interesting to hear what he had to say about relations between our two countries. From what I've read, he's sincerely interested in Cuba and Cubans." But I knew what Teseo was thinking. *Any association Regina has with the Enemy will go in MY file, and I'll never be able to get an exit permit.*

Strangely enough, after Parmly left the premises and Fuster went back to painting, Teseo had his own regrets. "I should have given him my card, in case he needs a good driver and a tour guide," he said, in total contradiction to what he expressed earlier, but by now I was getting used to all the contradictions in Cuba, political and personal.

(Later I would go back to my hotel and try to find a way to contact Michael Parmly by phone, but the U.S. Special Interests Section was not even listed in the Havana telephone directory, and I didn't have the energy or time to pursue this particular path of inquiry.)

Meanwhile, there we were, on Fuster's patio. Fuster himself was in his studio upstairs, and his son, Alex, came out to meet us. Alex was very good-looking, short and stocky, probably in his thirties, with dark hair and bright black eyes. He was a doctor by profession, but he no longer practiced medicine since he could make more money by acting as an agent for his father. Speaking English fluently, Alex served us a *cafecito* and showed us around Fuster's domain, starting with the upstairs. The stairway, of course, was paved with ceramics.

Fuster sat on a chair in the hallway working on a painting. He had the same build as his son, but his eyes were bright blue. The upstairs was being renovated, and a huge kitchen and dining room, along with living quarters, were taking shape. Every square inch of wall space was covered with paintings of Cuban motifs: the island in the shape of a crocodile, people smoking cigars, roosters, women with lopsided breasts, a caricature of Fuster himself.

Fuster was obviously busy, so we retreated to the lower rooms, where Teseo and I began looking at the artist's canvases. They covered every wall, were piled up on the floor, and filled dresser drawers. I finally chose a painting I particularly liked. It had to be wrapped and properly documented in order to take it out of the country, and Fuster told us to drop by later in the afternoon. Teseo, playing tour guide, had more places to show me, and by the time we returned to Fuster's, I was wilting from the heat.

Now that I'd made a purchase, Fuster became more animated. He had an infectious smile, a flirtatious manner, and a twinkle in his eyes. As if on cue, someone put on an Elvis Presley recording (in honor of my nationality, I suppose). Fuster took my hand and led me in a dance around the swimming pool. He was wearing only a bathing suit. I kicked off my sandals and we bopped around barefoot, singing and dancing to Elvis. We hugged each other, and he positioned me on his lap. We both laughed. "I'm glad you're a woman," he said.

"I'm glad you're a man," I responded. Fuster's grandson ran up at that moment, and they played a game of pushing each other into the pool. I grabbed my camera and took a few action shots of Fuster flailing his arms and legs before he splashed down.

"You must come to my birthday party," he announced. "August 30. I'm turning sixty."

"What would you like from America for your birthday?" I knew full well I wouldn't be able to come, although it was tempting to try. I imagined sitting at a table in that beautiful house, surrounded by friendly people, with the rum flowing, and lots of laughter.

"A bottle of Scotch," he said, without hesitation.

By now Alex had my painting all rolled up and wrapped with the proper documentation for Customs, and it was time to head out.

"I'll send you the photos," I promised.

"Great," said Alex. "We plan to put up all the photos people give us on the wall."

There were hugs all around, and Teseo and I waded through the urchins hanging around the entrance and went back to the car. On another trip, I would see Fuster again and give him his birthday present, a little belatedly. I'm not sure he even remembered me at that point, but he pretended he did.

Back in Havana, I realized that I had been neglecting Natasha. I asked her to come to dinner with me, leaving Teseo behind to babysit. She and I needed time for girl talk, a chance to bond.

There was entertainment in the restaurant, and two professionals, a man and a woman, were dancing salsa around the room, twirling between the tables. The woman was ebony black. Her rear end was a thing of beauty, enormous and jutting out like a ledge. In Cuba, this was considered a sign of beauty, something to be envied. Natasha sighed. "I wish I could borrow her ass for just one day, so I could walk down the street and see the attention I'd get." The dancers beckoned the audience to join them. There was no way we were going to embarrass ourselves, even though we both liked to dance.

As I walked to the elevator in the hotel, one of the young security guards approached me to practice his *piropo* in English. This was a form of flattery that a man gave to a woman, an art form. "You are so beautiful," he told me. "You have a wonderful light in your eyes!" He must have been thirty years younger than I. "Are you married? Yes? Oh, I am heartbroken!" He touched his heart and looked up at me through lustrous eyelashes. Not bad. I laughed, complimented him on his English, told him I was jealous of his long eyelashes, and bid him good-night. It was all a harmless game, good for the ego. Cuban men weren't afraid to flirt; no one was going to charge them with sexual harassment. There was always the chance that they might find a foreigner to help them out. But I was already taken.

XIV

Refrigerators and Religion

My friend, Orlando, was a great source of information about Cuba, and we often had long, philosophical discussions about everything from poetry to political theory. An American friend, Molly, and I were invited to dinner at his house, and Teseo was acting as our driver and translator.

Driving past the U.S. Special Interests Section along the Malecón, we got a glimpse of the ticker-tape that ran across the front of the building, carrying messages of freedom from Martin Luther King's speeches and detailing the contents of the free, public-school lunches in Miami. This in-your-face provocation prompted the Cubans to dig up a parking lot and come up with supposedly scarce building materials to erect a wall of black flags, blocking the American message from view to pedestrians and drivers. As we passed this, Teseo said, "Do you know what Cubans call those flags? The Berlin Wall."

Teseo often looked depressed, with an indescribable sorrow in his face, and tonight he seemed to be in a particularly bad mood. We zigzagged through the streets, avoiding the potholes. "The whole area looks like it's been bombed," he snarled. "Do you know what Cubans call Havana? Baghdad!"

Molly sighed and gave her standard answer to all the problems in Cuba. "Yes, the American embargo is terrible."

Teseo's face took on an expression of barely-disguised disdain, but sitting in the back seat, Molly didn't notice. I said nothing.

Orlando's house was quite small; in fact, his garage doubled as a living room, even with his car parked in it. The kitchen, however, had space for a big, round table, and we all congregated there with his wife and children. Molly and I were put to work peeling vegetables and grating cheese. Teseo lurked in the background, pretending he wasn't part of the scene, the better to observe it. He absented himself frequently to smoke a cigarette outside.

Orlando, a good-looking man in his fifties, had an advanced degree and held an important position in Havana. I was shocked when I first met him to see that he was missing a couple of front teeth. Once we became friends, he told me what happened. "During the Special Period I lost fifty pounds and my teeth went bad. Here it costs nothing to have a tooth pulled, but it costs money to have a crown put on, and I can't afford it."

Orlando made about fifteen dollars a month from his important position. His wife worked as an engineer, so together they earned about thirty dollars a month, and out of that they had to pay for food, water, electricity, gas for the car, prescription medicines, their telephone, and any upgrades they wanted to make to their house. So dinner for us must have broken the bank—pasta with a rich tomato sauce containing a small amount of hamburger, steamed carrots, and cheese and mango for dessert.

Orlando, a religious man, said grace before we eat. We complimented his wife on her cooking. She laughed. "We do the best we can without a refrigerator."

"But you have one," I commented, gesturing toward the ancient General Electric that took up space against the wall.

"Oh, that old thing. It lasted for over ten years, but now it's broken, and we can't afford to fix it. It's kind of hard, not having a refrigerator in this climate."

Molly and I looked at each other. Hadn't we been hearing about all the Chinese refrigerators being given to the Cuban people by the government?

"Yes, it's true," Orlando admitted. "The government will give you a new refrigerator, but only if you exchange your old one, which has to be in perfect working condition. The motor on ours is broken, and I'm not good at fixing things." Molly and I shook our heads in disbelief. How very un-Cuban, not to be able to fix something. Most Cuban men have had to become repairmen out of necessity. Orlando continued, laughing sheepishly. "If I pay someone to fix it, then I can exchange it for a new one, and it will cost only three hundred dollars."

"Wait a minute. I thought it was free."

"Well, almost. It's a good deal, because if I had to buy it on the world market, it would cost a lot more." Orlando smiled behind his mask, the mask that many Cubans wore. Did we get the joke? This explanation about the free refrigerator suddenly made sense to me. I had come a long way in understanding the *doble moral*, the two-faced double-talk that was a necessary survival tool in Cuba. I was learning to read between the lines.

"Why don't we just go into one of the dollar stores and buy you one?" To little-old-capitalist me this seemed logical, the easiest way to *resolver* the problem. If Molly and I and other friends of Orlando pooled our money, we could do it, although the refrigerator would cost a fortune in the Cuban convertible store, probably double what we'd pay in the U.S.

Orlando cringed at the suggestion. "I'm afraid the neighbors might notice the delivery." In other words, someone might get jealous and make trouble for him. All refrigerator deliveries had to be officially approved by the head of the Committee for the Defense of the Revolution.

Molly and I did eventually put our heads together, and we figured out a plan to get Orlando and his family a refrigerator. I won't go into the details of how we all accomplished this. He never officially acknowledged our effort; he would have had to do so by email, which was monitored. A year later, sitting with him on a wall outside my hotel, Orlando mentioned in passing that he now had a small refrigerator. "It's a very long, funny story," he whispered, but our friends were about to arrive, so there was no time for him to explain.

To this day I'm waiting to hear the story about how Orlando got his refrigerator. I'm sure he would tell it with a lot of animation, and we would laugh hysterically at the absurdity of life on Planet Cuba. Perhaps some day, during our lifetimes, he'll even be able to write it down for future generations, who will marvel at the Cuban government's interpretation of the word "free."

After dinner Orlando asked us, "Would you like to see my old house? It's been turned over to my pastor for use as a home church. I had a seven-year legal battle with the government over this." The house used to be the home of a deceased relative of Orlando's, who willed the house to the church, and the government challenged this. Having title to a house in Cuba didn't actually mean ownership of the land; it meant the right to live in the house, as long as the government let you. Buying and selling property was not legal, so Cubans often engaged in a *permutar*, exchanging one house for another. If they traded up they paid the seller money, under the table, or they could make money by trading down.

Orlando's home church was just down the street and around the corner from where he lived. Inside we met the charismatic young pastor. "We prayed for God to send us someone, and he came to lead our congregation. Now we have many people joining the church," said Orlando. The room was large, filled with folding chairs set in rows, about 200 of them. There were living quarters in the back of the house, for the pastor and his family. As we chatted, people wandered in and out.

I noticed a case at the front of the room that had brightly colored cardboard houses on display. It was crafted by a member of the congregation and was beautifully done. There were no people in this embellished street scene, only the housing, which appeared to be a dream of what housing should look like. Orlando explained that this represented the New Jerusalem.

The pastor suddenly challenged Molly and me: "What about you? Do you go to church? What religion are you?"

We were taken aback. "Buddhist," she replied.

"Jewish, but I don't practice. I was raised Unitarian."

"Jews are really the chosen people of God," the pastor assured me. "They always adapt and survive. They learn other languages."

Teseo, who was accompanying us, walked out in disgust at this point, mumbling something about having to smoke. Molly and I couldn't be that rude. I knew that evangelical Christianity was making a big comeback in Cuba, and I was happy that Orlando, for whatever reason, trusted me enough to share this part of his personal life with me. We had had discussions about religion, and he knew how I felt about it: It wasn't for me. I thought behavior was more important than belief, and I never noticed that people who were religious behaved any better than those who weren't. Still, I wanted to understand what all this meant to Orlando, and what the role of the home church was in Cuban society.

"What kind of activities does the church engage in?" I inquired.

"Right now we have a special project dealing with alcoholism, which is a big problem, especially in the more rural areas."

Orlando interjected, "Even little boys are given alcohol to drink; they are supposed to be men. This is part of the problem of the *machismo* culture in Cuba."

"So does the church provide people with services that are not available from the government?"

The pastor recoiled in horror. "Not at all! But *aquí soy libre*." He touched his head and his chest. "*¡Aquí soy libre!*" he repeated, emphatically, to make sure I got it. *I am free in here.*

Teseo dropped Molly where she was staying, and on the way back to my hotel, I asked him why he was in such a foul mood. "It's because of Orlando's house; he deserves so much better."

"Raúl Castro gave him the house." Orlando once told me this with pride.

"Thanks a *lot!*" said Teseo, and this response contained so much sarcasm that I couldn't help but laugh at how stupid I was and how absurd the Cuban reality was. And once I started laughing, Teseo started laughing, and this release escalated to the point that we were roaring with laughter, so hard that tears were streaming down my cheeks. And at that point I wasn't sure if I was laughing or crying.

Out of Cuba

My husband, Ralph, and I were waiting in the Toronto airport for the flight from Havana to arrive. There it was, up on the board. It seemed unreal. I couldn't believe Teseo and his family were actually out of Cuba until I saw them with my own eyes, and I wanted them to see us as soon as they came through the door. Ralph and I were pressed against the railing right in front, along with other families eagerly awaiting relatives. I knew Teseo's flight has already arrived, because I saw people with plasticized baggage dribbling into the waiting area. Cubans liked to burglar-proof every piece of luggage when they traveled. But where were the particular Cubans we wanted to see?

Impatient, I called Teseo's cousin, who was waiting for them at home. "It just takes a long time," she reassured me. "Don't worry. They're probably being questioned by Canadian customs." And suddenly there they were, bursting through the doors. They saw us almost immediately, and their faces lit up with smiles.

Teseo and I embraced, and his first words to me were, "I'm free." He looked down reverently at the ground, Canadian soil.

"They can't touch you now," I said.

"They can't touch me now," he repeated.

As we went to collect their luggage, Ralph ran ahead to snap photos of this happy reunion. Natasha stopped at the restroom and came back amazed. "They have toilet paper!"

When we went to the parking lot to retrieve the van, their son said, "Look at all these new cars!" And as the parking attendant wished us a "good day" with a big smile, Teseo commented, "Everyone is so nice. You would never have that happen in Cuba. I knew things would be better here, but I didn't know how much better they would be. I really resent all their lies." I expected this reaction eventually, maybe after two weeks of being in Canada, just not so soon. But Teseo was a quick study. "I always knew they were lying," he added, referring to the Cuban government. "I just didn't realize the extent of the lie."

The plan was for them to stay in the basement apartment of Teseo's cousin until they got established. Teseo had expressed anxiety about the process of getting settled, and I kept telling him, "Don't worry; everything will fall into place once you get there. We can't really rehearse it ahead of time." Indeed, before the week was up, the family found an apartment, signed the lease, moved in, bought furniture, registered for government benefits, and set up checking accounts at two different banks. Ralph and I were amazed at how easy things were in Canada for new immigrants. It was hard to get into the country, but once in, things ran pretty smoothly. The lines were short, the government officials were efficient, and everything fell into place, just as predicted.

The only time we ran into a roadblock was at the Cuban Consulate, where Teseo and Natasha had to register in order to keep their passports renewed, so they could return to Cuba to visit family. "You cannot enter Cuba if you are Cuban-born without a Cuban passport, even if you become a Canadian citizen," Teseo explained. "So they make you renew it every two years, at the cost of 250 dollars. This is just another way to squeeze money from people."

Being in the consulate, waiting for the paperwork to be processed, was like being back in Cuba. The air-conditioning didn't work. People were sitting around on chairs that lined the room, fanning themselves and looking bored but resigned. On the wall were a photo of Fidel, a photo of Ché, and a map of Cuba. Copies of *Granma* were lying around on a table, and I picked one up to take a look. It seemed quaint, a relic from a past century. I don't remember exactly what the front-page article was about, but I do remember that my first reaction was to burst out laughing at the pitiable journalism.

"This is the worse newspaper I've ever seen," I remarked to no one in particular. "It's full of nonsense." But my spontaneous behavior wasn't a joke to the woman sitting next to me.

"Shhh!" she chastened, gesturing toward the ceiling. "Be careful. They are listening. Your friends might get into trouble." She whispered to me that she had lived in Canada for ten years and was at the consulate because she wanted to go back to Cuba to visit family. Sadly, for her, the long arm of Castro reached all the way to Toronto. But I heeded her advice. I had forgotten where I was for a minute. I had already lost my internal censor.

XVI

Dark Matter

On my last trip to Cuba, I was over at Teseo's sister's apartment, located about thirty minutes away from my hotel in Old Havana. She, her boyfriend, Mom, and I chatted into the wee hours, and she promised me I wouldn't need to call a cab to return later: Her neighbor had a car and would be happy to drive me. When the time came, she called him. He took one look at me and freaked out. Apparently, she didn't mention that I was a foreigner. To make matters worse, I stupidly joked, "*Sí, soy el enemigo,*" I'm the enemy. No one laughed.

There was a quick conference among the Cubans, and it was decided that the two women, both of us white, would get into the back seat. The two men, both *mulato*, would sit in front. "This way it will look like we're two Cuban couples, and the police probably won't stop us." We positioned ourselves in the car accordingly and sputtered off over the potholes toward the hotel. I quickly passed some money to the driver, hoping this would make him feel the risk was worth it. His old jalopy shuddered and creaked, no one conversed, and fearful thoughts popped into my head. *We're going to break down on the way. I'll never make it back to the hotel. I'll miss my plane. I'll be stranded here. And I'll get my friends arrested.* For the first time in all my trips to Cuba, I was seized with a panic that was physical. My heart beat faster. I had trouble breathing. My hands began to sweat, and my stomach contracted. I felt like yelling "I've got to get out of here!" And I realized at that moment that I could never return to the island.

I noticed a similar anxiety in Cubans when I least expected it. I saw it in the stooped shoulders and nervous smile of a friend who cautioned me not to speak aloud in public while he quickly whispered an anti-government sentiment; in the doctor who was embarrassed but nonetheless begged me for computer equipment and magazine subscriptions, and who wouldn't let me enter his house because he feared I might be struck by crumbling ceiling plaster. This same friend apologized for not answering a question in writing. "I couldn't answer your email, sorry. The dengue fever epidemic was really bad. People died, but it was a state secret."

Fear is the dark matter of the Cuban universe. You can't really see it, but you can observe its effect on the people around you. Sitting in that car, on the way back to the hotel, I finally felt its gravitational pull on my own heart.

Perhaps I was now, truly, "almost Cuban."

Epilogue

Over six years have passed since Teseo and his family landed in Toronto. He and Natasha have good jobs, the kids speak English fluently, and they have bought a house and car. There is a growing population of young Cuban families in Toronto who give each other support, pass on tips about Canadian society, and have weekly dinners. Teseo and Natasha led the way for other Cuban immigrants who followed them, including Teseo's sister and her son.

I have to admit I worried a bit about what form our friendship would take once Teseo and I accomplished our goal and he and his family were safely in Canada. Perhaps the thrill would be gone once we were outside the exotic context of Havana, and we would slip away from each other. I'm happy to report that this was not the case. Although we're still far away geographically, we have managed to visit in person, and it's easy to stay in touch by phone and email without that old fear of censorship. If I've learned anything at all from my experience, it's this: It's not the place that's important, it's the people.

After the family's first northern winter, I waited for the other shoe to drop, half-expecting they would tell me they wanted to return to Cuba. It never happened.

"Teseo, I thought you would hate the cold and snow. I certainly did, growing up in Minnesota."

"No, we've adapted, and the kids love it, even though they can't play outside a lot of the time."

"You guys are truly amazing."

"Hey, we're Cuban! You know, I have tough days when I'm discouraged and I come home tired. But I know that this is just life. Nothing is perfect. At least here I have the opportunity to succeed and grow, and so do my children. I feel reborn."

Natasha confirmed this. "He's even smiling in his photos now." She, herself, occasionally experienced a form of survivor guilt. "We have so much here, and our families in Cuba have nothing."

As our friendship evolved, Teseo confided more about his past life in Cuba. The stories trickled out; perhaps it was a matter of losing that internal censor, or maybe he was finally comfortable enough to share more of his truth with me. I hoped he would eventually write his autobiography, perhaps when he was older and could reflect on his life without feeling pain, or when he didn't have to work so hard to support his family. I imagined his narrative would be full of philosophy, insight, and humor.

I compiled the material for this book over a ten-year period, but I couldn't bring myself to write it until I knew the family was safely in Canada. I thought the story could interest Teseo's and Natasha's children at a future date. Maybe they would wonder how this American woman and her husband came into their lives and made themselves part of the family's history. Or maybe they would take me aside and ask me why their parents wanted to get out of Cuba.

I would tell them the truth: "They did it for you."

Acknowledgments

My husband, Ralph Anavy, has always been my anchor in a safe harbor. None of this could have happened without his support.

A special thanks to Tamim Ansary for believing that "the world needs this book," and to the folks in the S.F. Writers Workshop, who first heard the story and encouraged me.

Amir Valle, I am honored that you wrote the introduction to my book.

I would like to thank the following writers, editors, and friends, who took the time to read and comment on the manuscript, giving me invaluable advice:

Carolyn Light Bell, Peter Fahey, Linda Hawkins, Steve Hawkins, Ulises Marin Escoto, Dario M. Perez, Mary Jo Porter, Grisell D. Ramirez, Julieta Gutierrez Ramos, Alan Rinzler, Rick Schwag, and Victoria Zackheim.

Michael Larsen liked the story but told me, "Honestly, there isn't much of a market for this book." Realizing I needed a publisher in Florida, I was lucky to find Alejandro Ramos of Cognitio Books and Apps, which I wouldn't have done without Gustavo Rodriguez, who chose Cognitio for his own work.

Brian Latell sent my chapter on the Venceremos Brigade to the Cuban Affairs Quarterly Electronic Journal, which published it, and this gave me the confidence to continue writing about Cuba.

I thank my friends at Babalu Blog, who welcomed me into their booth at Cuba Nostalgia, and gave me their love, moral support, and coffee.

About the Author

Regina Anavy was born in Minneapolis and received an A.B. in French Literature from the University of California, Berkeley, in 1965. She worked with the Congress of Racial Equality on voter registration, was involved in the women's movement in Washington, D.C., and traveled to Cuba with the Fourth Venceremos Brigade in 1971. Anavy is the author and editor of *Larry's Letters*, a true story about a Jewish family in North Dakota (Hummingbird Press 2005). Her articles and essays have been published in magazines, anthologies, and newspapers.

As part of a worldwide community of translators for the *HemosOído* website, Anavy has translated works by Juan Juan Almeida, Laritza Diversent, Iván García, Pablo Pacheco, Luis Felipe Rojas, Ángel Santiesteban, and Amir Valle. Her translation of "The Joke of the 'New Man'" appeared on *The Huffington Post* website (2010). Her essay, *Counter-Revolutionary: 1971*, was published in Vol. 7, Issue 2, of the 2012 Cuban Affairs Quarterly Electronic Journal.

Anavy has worked as a legal assistant, business owner, and crime reporter. She presently is retired and volunteers as an adjudicator on a restorative justice project for the San Francisco District Attorney's office. She lives in San Francisco with her husband.

Earth edition

www.EarthEdition.org

42430067R00095

Made in the USA
Lexington, KY
21 June 2015